WELCOME
TO THE
ZOO

WELCOME TO THE ZOO

A Whistleblower's Memoir

by

LLOYD KRAAL

REGENT PRESS
Berkeley, California

ISBN 13: 978-1-58790-166-9
ISBN 10: 1-58790-166-8
Library of Congress Control Number: 2009-923601

ACKNOWLEDGEMENTS

I would like to thank my wife Sue for the love and support she has given me over the thirty years we have been together, and my three daughters for always believing in me. I appreciate that my father taught me to fight back, and my mother always loved me. My uncle Jim showed me how to be a carpenter and a man. My sister and two brothers still put up with me. It was the Dominican sisters of Our Lady of Mercy who taught me right from wrong. I am grateful to my editor, Leda Ciraolo, for helping me with this project; MG for her humor and input; and the numerous city employees who supported me during hard times. And a special thanks to Jean for her love and support throughout this journey. Thank you all.

Manufactured in the United States of America
REGENT PRESS
regentpress@mindspring.com
www.regentpress.net

Table of Contents

Prologue

A city like San Francisco

encompasses the very best of us and also lays bare the very worst of us. Corruption, thievery and shady backroom deals are more the norm than the exception. Every City and County of San Francisco department I have worked for in the last twenty years had million dollar scams. We have accepted this type of behavior in the corporate world and now we have become complacent when this same dishonesty and vice permeate the fabric of our public lives. San Francisco is no different than any other major American city in most ways. When a flaw is exposed in one of our leaders, department heads, or our city workforce, we don't act diligently to find an explanation or to separate that individual. Rather, those in power quickly circle the wagons and go into damage control.

The young mother who had her arms ripped to shreds by a Siberian tiger at the San Francisco Zoo was a victim of this institutionalized corruption, as was the dead teenager who had his head nearly ripped off by the same animal a year later. Two young men were left to fend for themselves as their bones were crushed and the flesh ripped from their bodies as the San Francisco Zoo staff ran for cover.

I wrote this book to expose the crime and corruption that underlie the fabric of our city. The senior staff of the zoo and their lawyers were warned the tiger grottos were not safe, long before the tiger escaped. They were told the tiger could reach through the bars, long before she did. I know this to be true because I told them. During the twenty years I spent working for the City and County of San Francisco I repeatedly encountered the same lies, accusations, and cover-ups I now see following the death and mauling of these young men. I wrote this book to explain how this tragedy happened, in the hope that it will not happen again. This is my story.

Although all of the events recorded in this book are true, the names of most individuals have been changed to shield their identities. Many of these events are a matter of public record in the form of news stories and court depositions, so interested parties may investigate these documents.

Chapter One

Welcome to the Zoo

As the siren's eerie bellow grew louder, I felt the sharp reeds along Lake Merced cut my face and hands as I frantically attempted to escape my pursuers. Suddenly, a loud, low voice ordered me to stop and come to the street. I looked behind me at the panic-stricken expressions on Peter Otis's and Mike Lawson's faces. I lost sight of them soon after, unable to see through the thick vegetation. I increased my speed and weaved through the razor grass with the agility and ease of the seasoned ten-year-old I was. I knew these shores very well; my father had taken my brother and me to Lake Merced for the trout season opening day to fish and explore for as long as I could remember. We would sleep over in the back of our Chevy station wagon the night before in order to obtain a good spot for the morning's first fishing. These fishing outings, and all outings, were always accompanied by whiskey drinking on my father's part—

usually a couple of half pints. Matter of fact, he drank straight out of the bottle at regular intervals throughout the night as we practiced our celebrity impressions.

I knew these reeds well. Alas, no matter how fast I could navigate through this maze of knife-like fronds, I could not escape San Francisco's finest. As I bolted through a clearing in the brush I came face to face with a huge blue figure. I squirmed to get away while his giant hands grasped my derby coat. Peter and Mike were already in the cop car crying hysterically a few feet in front of me. In my pockets were two baby chicks I had volunteered to raise. Well, not exactly. I had stolen them from the San Francisco Children's Zoo across the street. They were not my first, but they were my last. Apparently, the staff had gotten tired of us making off with their charges. Meanwhile, we were having trouble with our own chicken program at home. Home was 54 Palmdale, about two miles away, in Daly City, California. I had already made off with a little bantam rooster we named Fergie. I got him from the area outside the zoo—a great critter gathering ground for ten-year-olds. I had made off with probably two or three baby chicks previously, but something kept getting in the cage I had built in my backyard and eating them, so it was time to restock.

My mind was jolted back to the present as the ambulance sped by me, siren screaming. December 22, 2006. I turned from Lake Merced and gazed down the circular drive that I had so many times used to enter my beloved zoo. The loud squawk on my zoo radio brought me painfully back to reality, "Lea is loaded into the ambulance and they have exited the zoo." I bid goodbye to the 911 emergency operator I had on my zoo cell phone, exchanged some pleasantries, and slowly walked to the Lion House. About six minutes had elapsed since I first heard the security guard's frantic whimpering of a code one on my zoo radio. "Code one, code one. Lea's down at the Lion House, Lea's down at the Lion House, oh my God, we need an ambulance at the Lion House." Jen Bears was the next voice I heard on the radio, attempting to ascertain if the animal was loose. The next voice I heard was Todd Dennis informing the caller he was on his way to the Lion House. At 2:21 p.m. on December 22, 2006, I called 911. At first the operator asked me if I was kidding. I assured her I was not and gave her my name and position at the zoo and the nature of the emergency. I informed the operator we had a female keeper attacked and injured at the Lion House and we needed an ambulance right away. Todd Dennis told me to make sure they came in the Skyline entrance closest to the Lion House. An extremely calm and professional woman's voice began to ask me some questions about Lea's condition. I informed the operator I was not with the injured keeper and offered to let her go so she could speak to someone at the Lion House. She had no one else, so I was attempting to relay information from Todd Dennis. When I radioed Todd again, he had not yet reached the "House."

That is the name "Lion House Jon" called this 1940's era art deco building where I had spent so many of my childhood days watching the lions and tigers and the old grizzled fellow who took care of them in the 1960's and 1970's. I later found out his name was Cedric Case. Cedric Case had some type of ape or baboon in the house at the time, and during the countless hours I spent in this very special place I saw a lot of things. This baboon or mandrill was very protective and testy. Consequently, kids and all types of cruel people would tease this animal. When Cedric noticed his charge in distress he would calmly stroll over in full force, long, wild, grey hair matching an unkempt beard and his blue-grey zookeeper uniform.

Almost always the culprits would back away, trying to blend into the large crowd these feedings would draw. Cedric Case would put his arm around this creature and the creature in turn would put his arm around Cedric. Then Cedric would ask who was bothering him. Every time that ape would point right at the detractors and scream, jump up and down, and generally make a huge ruckus. Then Cedric Case would give a lecture to the guilty, and anyone else in earshot, on the pathetic type of individual who would tease and upset this wonderful creature, caged and imprisoned so the public could learn and look at this unique animal.

As I walked down the circular drive towards the Lion House, an animal keeper, a pretty mother with black hair and Italian features, approached and spoke tersely to me regarding several police cars stuck in the mud near the tiger attack site. I ignored her attitude and summoned the maintenance crew via zoo radio and asked Jimmy and Renee to meet me at the Lion House. They were already there. I directed them to remove the squad cars from the mud. They could not quite figure out how to do it without damaging the cars. Jimmy thought it might be best that we pick the cars up with the forklift. I wasn't quite sure if he wanted to damage the police cars or if he was just not too bright. So I spent thirty minutes or so coordinating the police car rescue.

The rock in my stomach grew harder and larger as I felt panic welling up inside me. Four months ago, shortly after I accepted the position of Maintenance Supervisor for the San Francisco Zoo, Willy Ramirez, the Operations Director at the zoo and the apparent second in command, radioed me: "Maintenance Lloyd. This is Ops. One; come to my office." Willy Ramirez explained to me that the keepers were lazy and felt entitled to more attention than they were due.

Jon Realdo, the Lion House keeper in charge of the tigers and lions, had been calling me earlier that day. Like most of the keepers, he was looking for some much-needed improvements to his work area. I liked Jon Realdo, especially after he said he was praying for me. My sister Kim also informed me that he was involved in some type of community effort in her hometown to save a neighbor's house from a landslide danger. I trusted Jon and felt him to be a good man. I did not feel that from Willy Ramirez. Willy was a small, nervous young man who appeared to be about eighteen. I later found out he was thirty. Willy was a talker—mostly about himself and his accomplishments.

Jon Realdo was very tall. He would lean over then fold his large arms across his barrel chest as he explained to me the shortcomings of the current management. I would listen for a short time, and then usually I would get another call for maintenance. I was extremely busy at The San Francisco Zoo. I was also racked with guilt over Lea's mishap, and I should not have been. I put my job on the line every day I reported to the zoo, which was seven days a week.

After the police cars were unstuck and Lea had been taken to the hospital, my mind went floating back further, to the first day I went to work for the City and County of San Francisco.

Chapter Two

Dog Patch

It was a sunny spring morning

in 1985 when I walked into the cable car shop on 22nd and Minnesota Street, in an area of San Francisco known as Dog Patch. Dog Patch was a section off Third Street in an area of the city that was generally unsafe. As I drove past the Local 483 carpenters' union I smiled, although it looked deserted and abandoned. Local 483 was a very lively union hall. They used to call it Cahill's Local because most of its members were carpenters working for Cahill Construction, a particularly tough outfit to work for. Sometime in the late 70s I had a job with Cahill; we were working in the South of Market area on a nondescript parking garage of some sort—all concrete and steel. There must have been three hundred carpenters on that job. Every Friday Cahill would lay off twenty-five or so, and then hire twenty-five more on Monday. I asked the unpleasant Chinese foreman the reason for this. He told me it was to keep the rest of us on our toes, and I better get back to work or I could be next.

Tug Boat Annie's Bar and Grill on Third and Minnesota marked the entrance to my new world. The docks were close by and a sprinkling of dock worker restaurants and drinking establishments were scattered about. The Southern police station was down the street; it resembled a building under siege with its caged windows and chain-linked perimeter. The Bayview District, a notoriously violent and crime-ridden neighborhood, was a few blocks down the street. Gang killings, gunshots and assaults were commonplace in this part of town. I turned onto 22nd Street; an old Victorian cottage advertised Friday's fish fry for $5.95. I parked my white Monte Carlo next to a beautiful new shop building with a wall of tinted glass a hundred feet long, thirty feet high stonewalls, and an expensive Standing Seam red metal roof. I walked past a man in a shop coat chatting with what appeared to be a prostitute smoking a cigarette at the door of a large, old motor home. Two more workers in blue Muni jumpsuits appeared to be buying drugs from two men in a worn Oldsmobile. Another fellow was lying on the large, well-manicured lawn. His round red face angled towards the bright morning sun; he wore a heavy brown oversized leather jacket. It was only about 50 degrees. I made my way to the huge roll-up door with steel tracks leading into the building.

The excitement was growing inside me. Finally I thought: I am here. I have made it; my troubles were over. No more lay offs, no more backaches, no more surly construction workers: a city job! I could barely contain myself; this meant better conditions, steady work, and a regular paycheck. Even though it was quite a bit less than I was used to, it was a career. No telling how far I could go, I thought. If I could rise to a superintendent like I did on the outside, what lay ahead of me here? The two men who interviewed me, Len the carpenter foreman and Ronald Greene, a manager, seemed like decent men, but neither one knew much about building. I was sure to surpass men like these in no time.

I was only twenty-eight, but the last few years had been hard on the outside. My back and neck were causing me a great deal of pain. I could no longer perform the heavy construction work I could when I was twenty. I had had numerous injuries, countless doctors' appointments, years of chiropractic care, physical therapy and prescription drugs. No doctor was able to tell me what was wrong, but they all agreed I was too young to have this bad of a back. It was my bad back that actually brought me to the city. And it was my bad back that led me out as well.

Matt O'Reily

Matt O'Reily died of AIDS. I had a great deal of affection for Matt, and his father, William O'Reily, appreciated this. Matt O'Reily spent most of his life in an alcohol and drug induced haze. He was a fun guy though, and I liked him. Because of his habits he was discharged from the army, even though he wanted to stay. Matt had a hard time keeping a job, as you might guess.

As my family was growing I would many times work "side jobs": weekend work, at night, after my regular job, or in between carpenter jobs. I would include Matt in these endeavors and always split the profits with him. Matt lived with his father William and mother, Bet O'Reily. William and Bet lived around the block from my father's house and Matt was staying with them, even though he was twenty-five or twenty-six years old. I was around the same age with a wife and two children to support. William and Bet were desperately hoping Matt would follow my lead and move out on his own. My friend Matt never did leave, except when he would spend the weekends in a dive motel in the Tenderloin with some hookers, some drugs, and alcohol.

I was working as a construction superintendent at a high-rise site on Van Ness Avenue when Keiren O'Reily called me. Keiren was William's youngest: a friend of my younger brother, Bart. "Hey, my dad says the city is going to hire a bunch of carpenters. They are giving the test at his work; if you want some info come by or give William a call. My dad says you won't have trouble with your back working for the city," Keiren said over the phone. I thanked Keiren and asked about Matt. Keiren said he hadn't seen him in a while, but he thought he was working as a security guard or something. A few days later after an argument with a co-worker I went to see William O'Reily. William O'Reily was a smallish man—rather slim, almost too thin, kind of a sickly slim. William didn't look well, he had that Irish complexion: very pale with freckles, translucent skin stretched tightly over high cheekbones, and a protruding chin. And he was nearly bald. William looked like he had been through the ringer. I greeted William in front of the house. We talked some in his garage; I asked about Matt. We exchanged pleasantries and talked about the city job. William told me to go down to City Hall and fill out a job card. When they opened the carpenter job up I would hear about it by mail. I thanked William and went home. The next day I went down to City Hall in San Francisco and filled out the job card.

The site superintendent's job I had was across the street from the city office. I got off at 3:30 p.m. and the office didn't close till 4:30 p.m., so I had some time. In this office they had three huge books all filled with city jobs, their responsibilities, and their pay. When you found one you wrote the "class number" down on the courtesy card, bought a stamp from the machine, self-addressed the card, and handed it back to the person behind the counter. I found "carpenter," followed instructions, and completed my task in about ten minutes. I also saw "zookeeper," so I filled one out for that as well. I proudly walked my completed cards to the two ladies at the counter. I greeted one and tried to make conversation as she looked my cards over. She ignored my greeting and flashed me a bored look. Her nametag said Ms. Brown. The next day I returned to my job; we poured one hundred and fifty yards of concrete at the high rise on Van Ness. About one hundred and forty five more than I poured in the eighteen years I worked for the city.

In about a month I got my card back from the city. The carpenter job was opening up and I needed to fill out a city application and get it to the city office by next week. I did this and finished the high rise on Van Ness. I went to work for my friend Devin Black as a construction superintendent and had my best year ever. I bought a house in Petaluma. I had a barbeque pit in the garden, and my wife worked at her sister's restaurant on the weekends. We had some extra money and a lot of pets in the backyard. I felt like I had really made it.

I lost track of Matt O'Reily, but remained in touch with Keiren and William. I got a letter from the City and County of San Francisco asking me to test for the carpenter's job. I called William and told him about the letter. I asked William what I should expect. William told me, "There should be a little of everything: some layout, some tool identification, and work on a table saw." I was a little nervous about the table saw. I had been a carpenter for about ten years now, and I had only used a table saw a couple of times, mostly in apprentice school. I had worked mostly large-scale jobs with a lot of concrete forms or framing. As of late I was supervising. So I thought I should bone up. I got my books out. I trimmed out a couple of windows using a table saw. I wasn't worried——carpentry came easy to me.

I was so excited that I arrived an hour early to the Port of San Francisco Pier 46B maintenance yard. I had my hard hat on, my hand tools, and a big grin. I was only twenty-seven, but I felt I had been through a war. The last three years I had gotten married, had two kids, and bought a house. My mother was threatening suicide again. My father's diabetes caused by his alcoholism had brought him near death several times. I felt like I was due a break. I didn't notice much at the shop, but as men do, we were all looking each other over pretty good. I finished the test all right. I thought I had some trouble on the table saw, but a nice old guy helped me out. I said "See ya later," to William and went back to my job. I worked another year for Devin Black. I did side jobs, but I never saw Matt O'Reily again.

Chapter Three

Woods Carpenter Shop

I came to a metal door with a plaque above it that read: Woods Carpenter Shop. This was the City of San Francisco's cable car maintenance shop. I rang the bell; a deafening horn blew, the door buzzed, and I was in. A round hairy man, with rotten teeth and very bad breath, walked quickly over to me as I entered the carpenter shop. He introduced himself as Jim McMan. He thrust his meaty palm my way and vigorously shook my hand. I asked Jim if Len was around. Jim replied, "No, he is off sick or something. You want Bob! He's outside sleeping. He's the boss now. It's a long story—I am sure someone will fill you in." The phone rang and Jim walked fast to the origin of the ring. He had a bad limp. The Asian carpenter laughed out loud as Jim scrambled to the phone.

The shop was a cathedral-like building with a fifty-foot ceiling, a wall of tinted windows, and two unfinished cable cars on tracks in the middle of the work area. Huge saws and woodworking machines were everywhere. Well-made workbenches were scattered about, with men at each one. I milled about, feeling uncomfortable. Just then I heard a voice from behind some lumber, "Don't just stand there; let me introduce you around." A sickly man who looked like he might be seventy years old, with a cigarette in his mouth, sauntered over to me and said, "I'm Billy Crown; you must be the new carpenter. Don't mind these guys—they are all pushed out of shape that you did better on the test than them," and Billy laughed hard. A strong odor of alcohol wafted through the air. I looked down to see a sixteen-ounce Rainer ale can in Billy's left hand. "You know these guys practiced for the carpenters' test for almost a year right here in the shop. I don't think any of them got higher than number sixty." Billy laughed hard and the liquor smell filled the air.

We walked over to a huge milling machine. "This is Von." A somewhat handsome, stout Latin man slowly turned off the machine, and removed his ear protection. Von was about my height, and close to my age, but he weighed probably fifty pounds more. A huge gut stretched his leather smock. Von gave me the once over, nodded, and stated he was ranked number forty-six, and he only practiced for about six months. He said, "These other guys made so many drawers they had to start hiding the waste so to not attract attention." Having heard this, the Asian carpenter yelled, "Fuck you, Von." Another older guy came over and introduced himself as Lon.

Now Lon looked even closer to death than Billy. Lon's

gut looked out of place; he was very slender, but his mid-section was huge and his coloring was bad. His eyes were bloodshot and he smelled more like booze than Billy. Suddenly, I heard another voice from behind me. I was startled and a little overwhelmed by this time. "What do we have here? The new guy. You know you shouldn't even be here," a short, lanky young man with watery eyes and a cigarette in his hand exclaimed, all the time staring directly into my eyes, which made me feel that he really didn't like me.

Just then, I heard someone say, "That's enough. Get back to work." I turned to meet the voice and sure enough, it was the sunbather from outside. I recognized this man as one of the men from the carpenters' test at the port. "You must be Lloyd," he said. "Yes, I am the new carpenter."

"I'm Bob, the carpenter supervisor. I see you have met some of the men. Why don't you and Billy put this plywood away. I have got some errands to run; Billy will show you around." Then he was off, out the door.

Billy mumbled something, then walked to a stack of 3/4 plywood. He stood there for a few seconds, finished his beer, and lit another smoke. He offered me one. I took it and we had a smoke. "You know that little prick never did a day's work for the Muni when he was a carpenter, and has stayed drunk for as long as I've known him. Things are changing, that's for sure. Well, you ready? Let's get this plywood in the rack." I removed my jacket, set my paperwork down, and grabbed the other end of the ply-wood sheets. We worked in unison for about ten minutes.

I started to sweat and felt pretty good about myself. Suddenly, Billy dropped his end and nearly tore my arm off. "Hey! Jesus...fucking...Christ, what are you trying to do, kill me for fuck's sake? You better get something straight right now, kid. You have twenty years to get this plywood in these racks; after we get this stack put away there will be another stack, then another stack. No one likes a show-off; if you want to get along here you just better slow down and don't be a fucking hot shot. Now it's coffee time. I am going to get a beer; you want one?" It was 9:30 a.m. I said no thank you. "Well, when I get back I will show you how to make coffee. In the meantime since you're so fucking eager, finish this fucking plywood." The Asian carpenter laughed again. The lanky guy stared with a smile as I finished the plywood. Billy came back from the store, drank three tall beers, then went to sleep in the corner of the shop.

Lon made the coffee. After a silent and tense twenty minutes in the break room, Bob showed me a locker I could use and gave me a field sketch. "You think you could build this?" Bob asked. The shop stopped and listened in silence. I said, "Sure!" I looked the drawing over; there were three projects, and they appeared to be some kind of carnival games. The shop guys looked at each other, nodded, and went back to work. I separated the different sizes of lumber, made a list of the components, and started cutting my pieces. By the end of the day I had one almost complete. Bob came over and was obviously excited. "Wow you are fast! My church is always asking me for these kind of things." Just then an older man in a blue work suit came in and spoke to Bob quietly. Bob nodded and told me to put six sheets of half-inch plywood in the man's truck. I complied. The worker handed me a paper bag and thanked me. I thanked him back and brought the bag to Billy, who was operating a large saw. When he saw me coming he shut down the saw and slowly removed his eye wear and ear protection. Billy opened the bag and pulled out a half gallon of cheap brandy.

"This will help! C'mon kid, I'll show you how things work around here." We went up the stairs to the break room. Billy opened the cabinet doors under the 25" color TV and slipped the brandy next to about twenty-five other bottles of liquor. I said, "Wow! You guys like brandy." Billy laughed. Billy said, "When someone gets materiel for a home project or a government job they give us a jug; that's how it works. Don't give anything away, kid, unless you get something in return."

Billy went to the cupboard, set out a handful of shot glasses, took out an open brandy bottle and set it on the table. "We always have a drink before we go home. You better join us or the men won't trust you." It was now about 3:45 p.m. in the afternoon of my first day as a City and County carpenter. I was sure the police would be here soon. And we would all be arrested.

I worked on the carnival games for a couple more days, had coffee at ten o'clock and brandy at three-thirty, driving home drunk several times. After a few weeks I was informed that on Thursdays the shop had lunch at the bar on the corner: the famous Tug Boat Annie's. They served steak sandwiches to the stevedores and had lingerie shows that seemed more like strip shows to me. The girls who put on the "lingerie" shows were "Lizzy's Lovely Ladies." I knew these girls from my Daly City neighborhood and had gone to high school with Lizzy's brother. Still, none of this was new to me, so hey, when in Rome....

A strange turn of events was occurring, unbeknownst to me. As the weeks moved on, Bob, the foreman, began to show an uncomfortable interest in me. Bob would ask me to stay at the bar after he would rudely instruct the men to return to work. He would then watch another show and order us another round of drinks. We would regularly return much past 1:00 p.m., usually intoxicated. Bob would get in the truck and leave. I started to receive some angry outbursts from my co-workers.

As it turned out, the men hated Bob for taking Len's job. The story I got from Billy was that Len Tinman, the man who hired me, was the temporary carpenter shop foreman for nearly twenty years. He and Billy were old friends from the outside. A civil service test was given for the position of carpenter supervisor; the first one in nearly fifteen years. Bob received a higher score than Len, so he was chosen for the job of carpenter supervisor. Len was devastated and took some time off to show his frustration. Lon was some relation to Len Tinman and the short, lanky guy, who really didn't like me, was Lon's stepson: he was called Lenny. Now, Lenny was a beauty: he had blue eyes and he looked like he was maybe black. A nice looking guy, but very angry. He drank a lot, he only came to work about three days a week, and those days he was very hung over and would drink beer all day. Lenny developed an extremely strong dislike for me that I could not fully understand. Lenny lived in the projects close to the shop. He invited me there one day after work, I think so he could throw me out, which he did after accusing me of some verbal indiscretion.

This was 1985 and city carpenters made about $40,000 a year plus benefits. I owned a house and was raising two daughters. My wife worked a couple days a month, and I was even able to save some money. So, I asked him why he lived in government housing. I think he took offense so he kicked me out of his apartment. It was never spoken of at work. He might not have remembered.

Jimmy Lee was a Chinese furniture maker from Hong Kong and an alcoholic. Jimmy was a decent fellow, but he really should not touch alcohol. Jimmy's face and neck would turn a deep, unhealthy red after just one drink. He then would have three or four more, mostly on these Thursday lunchtime outings. Most of the time Jimmy Lee was friendly, although his English was bad. When he had the heats you could not understand him and he would hug and maul, drooling and spitting all over his unlucky co-worker. Von Peralta looked Latin and took the train from San Jose. Von would brag about the abuse, both verbal and physical, he inflicted on his wife during her menstrual period if she did not stay with her mother. Von had been a door maker at his former job and was some type of relative to Len Tinman as well. Von was a tough guy; when he drank, he spoke of the ass whoopings he had given out over the years. Von definitely looked like he could give one, but it was my experience the real tough guys don't speak of it.

About a month after I started, Adam Smith came back to the cable car shop after recovering from some type of injury. I was very happy to see Adam the Black Smith—that is what he called himself—again. Adam would explain it this way: my name is Adam Smith. I am a blacksmith and I am black, so I am Adam the Black Smith. A couple years previously Adam had given me the performance part of the City and County's carpenter exam. I was not too familiar with the ancient table saw at the Port of San Francisco's carpenter shop, or any other table saw for that matter, and he almost stopped and disqualified me. But Adam let me finish and I scored in the top 15%. I liked Adam; he was seventy years old, straight and strong, honest and sober. I did not leave his side. This was a challenge sometimes, because Adam was not only a blacksmith, but a minister as well. I received many hours of religious teachings, which I welcomed in place of the alternative. Unfortunately, Adam's health started to waver. Jimmy, Von, and Lenny, despite years of practice, did badly on the City and County of San Francisco's carpenter test. They placed low on the hiring list.

Things were becoming clear now. Ms. Brown, the personnel analyst at Muni, urged me not to take the position at the cable car shop. Ms. Brown told me over and over I would be foolish to take this position as it was a temporary appointment and would only last a week or two. Ms. Brown worked hard for Jimmy, Von, and Lenny. I thought she would not process my acceptance. Finally, I had to insist and question her motives. Ms. Brown was also some type of relation to Lenny. One summer afternoon, while Lenny was enjoying his third tall Budweiser in the back of the carpenter shop, I happened by Von, Jimmy and Jim "Dragon Breath" McMan consoling Lenny regarding some mysterious impending lay off, and how the addition of a new carpenter with a much higher ranking might affect his job picture. "You know everything was fine 'til you got here." I stopped and smiled. I was twenty-eight years old. I wasn't tall, about 5'9". I weighed about 180 pounds. I was tan and muscular; I had been a carpenter since I was sixteen. I grew up on a construction site. My father was a violent American Indian/Irish ex pro-boxer with a drug and alcohol problem. He had left the family when I was fifteen and I spent the next ten years or so fighting my younger brother's battles, as well as my own. I had my own issues. They did not know, but I was not a great victim. I ignored the comment. "You know you don't even belong here; you should have listened to Ms. Brown." I said, "Ms. Brown—now I see." Jimmy Lee quickly rose from his chair, his face a bright scarlet, an ample supply of saliva streaming down his lips and chin.

Jimmy placed himself directly in front of me and began a tirade that I could not make out. After he had had his say, Von walked towards me. I stood my ground. The gang of four probably didn't realize I had been in this situation on more than one occasion. I had assessed the situation on my way over. I had identified possible defense aids in and around the immediate area and had already formulated a plan in the event one or more of these brave men decided to get froggy. I was not concerned. "You don't belong here!" Von shouted from several feet away. "Yeah, we been here for years. Building cable cars is specialized; that was what Ms. Brown was trying to tell you," shouted Lenny slouched in his chair. "You know, they are right, you shouldn't even be here," Bad Breath Jim added. The stench from Jim's mouth turned my stomach.

When I think back I wonder if I had walked away, if I had put my head down, apologized for being there, offered to quit, would that have made the next eighteen years less of a nightmare? I didn't walk away; I didn't offer to quit; I didn't apologize. That was not in me. My father taught me never to start a fight but never to walk away from one either. And I never did: I never started a fight and I never walked away from one. By the time I got out of grammar school I had broken my hands many times fighting. I was a small child and, as you know, children are cruel, especially when your father is the town drunk and your mother weighs three hundred pounds. I got my assed kicked a thousand times. Something happened though: I learned how to fight—I mean dirty: kick in the teeth, punch in the throat, and knee you in the balls street fighting.

When I was twenty years old I was in a bar in North Beach with another carpenter when a stocky Vietnam vet knocked me off the bar stool. When I came to I left him and his friend in a bloody heap, unconscious and bleeding badly. The next morning I was fitted for casts on both hands. A year later I was at Candlestick Park one evening with my brother when a group of Chicago Cubs' fans spit in my face. I beat three of them unconscious. I am not proud of this. But I was confident in a few things as a twenty something, and one was self-defense.

So, I spoke up. I first told Jimmy to get out of my face. I told him he should quit drinking, that he turns purple and spits, and you can't understand a word he says. I told Lenny and Jimmy that they had a year to practice for the test and still failed—that's not my fault. I told them that I am not the one that didn't belong there. It was they who didn't belong there. I pointed at Jimmy and stated he was a furniture maker, not a carpenter. I looked at Von and told him he was a door maker trained to pull a lever, not a carpenter. I said, "And you, Lenny, you're a sheet rocker who only got the job from family. So the way I look at, the only one that belongs here is me." This sent Shit Breath Jim a limping and sat Jimmy down in a second. Von, being more accustomed to intimidating women, scurried on, claiming he had work to do.

Now, Lenny surprised me. He gathered himself together, got up, puffed out all one hundred and twenty-five pounds of himself and said, "You're not going to get my job," and steadied himself in front of me. I felt a calmness come over me and realized this battle was over. I kind of liked Lenny. He really was the only one with any courage. I told him I didn't want his job; I wanted my own job. I told him I needed this job for my family. I told him my family was counting on me. The city was looking for carpenters; I am a carpenter. They called me; I took the job; that's all. Lenny threw his hands up, gave me one of those I hate your guts looks, and stormed out.

Lenny didn't come to work for ten days after that. When I turned to go back to work, Bob had returned from another errand and was starring at me with a blank look. Len Tinman and Billy said, "Way to go kid," as I passed. Lon pretended not to see me.

Woods Carpenter Shop on 22nd and Minnesota was the accepted and official venue for all the Muni retirement parties. At about 9:00 a.m. on the day of the party things started getting underway. The heavy hitters, as Billy called them, had high balls. The rest of us started cleaning the shop. The tables were brought out, the paper covers were attached with tape, while the plaques and wood gifts were readied in the pattern shop by Jim, the pattern maker. It took me awhile, but I finally figured out what old crap mouth was supposed to be doing. He spent most of his time gossiping and starting trouble. But his real job was very interesting, and if you could stand him, his work was impeccable.

The barbeque was fired up and at about 11:00 a.m. the guests started arriving: old men and their wives, mostly white men. It was potluck, buffet style, with a full bar and plenty of drunk people by 2:00 p.m. I was standing next to the door having a smoke and drinking a beer when I heard a familiar voice. "Hey, Kraal, what the fuck are you doing here?" I turned and lo and behold, it was Donnie Bones, an old friend from the neighborhood. Now his name was not really Donnie Bones. His name was Donnie Jeter. Donnie had the unlucky experience of getting his ass kicked by a girl one night at Bianchini's Bar. Now, it wasn't exactly a fair fight, but still, getting your ass kicked by a girl should be avoided at all costs, even if she was a two hundred pound lesbian. Unfortunately for Donnie, that thirty seconds probably shaped the next thirty years of his life. But the name Bones came from a bartender at a tavern in Westlake, which is an area in Daly City where I grew up. Bones was the name of a very slender bartender who worked at the Westlake Pizza Parlor. This establishment was owned by a Greek man who apparently felt that the drinking restrictions did not apply to his tavern. Bless his heart, we drank there from the time we were eighteen or nineteen until we could get into the discos, then we came there less and less.

Donnie was a horrible drunk. He was the only child of an older couple that cruised the seven seas most of the time. Donnie had fast cars and plenty of spending money, which he crashed and spent on liquor, respectively. One evening Jerry Reynolds and I met Donnie at the Pizza Parlor for a couple of pitchers. As usual, Donnie got blind and legless drunk. As Jerry helped him to our car, Donnie was remembering, not fondly, his encounter with the female Ali. "You know, sometimes I wish I wasn't me," Donnie slurred. Jerry, having recently returned from a tour of duty in Germany, had a good sense of humor and a quick wit. I always liked that about Jerry. I said, "Well maybe we should call you 'Donnie I mean Bones.'" Jerry laughed hardily. From that night on, Donnie was either referred to as the guy who got his ass kicked by a girl, or "Donnie Bones."

There was another life changing event at Westlake Pizza Parlor for a teenage me and a man in his thirties.

Ryan Shashido lived up the block from me on Palmdale Avenue in Daly City. Ryan was part Irish and part Japanese. His father was a friendly giant of a man with white hair and his mom was a small Japanese woman. Ryan was big, like his father, with a huge head. Ryan Shashido still holds the field goal record for high school football. Ryan kicked a sixty-five yard field goal in a game against Lowell High School in 1971. Well, Ryan liked me, so he used to take me out drinking when I was fourteen or fifteen and Ryan was seventeen or eighteen. We would get a bottle of rum and some coke and drive around then eat pizza at the parlor.

One Friday night I was exceptionally drunk and leaning precariously against the counter at the pizza parlor. A man in his thirties was there with his family, and tripped on my foot. Believing I tripped him on purpose, the thirty-year old father of two unwisely grabbed me and began to throttle me about. I began to come around. Seeing double, maybe triple, I unleashed a short jab then a right cross, as I had been taught by my father in the ring in our basement. Down he went like a ton of bricks. Ryan Shashido, having seen this, elevated me immediately to a status I was not accustomed to: I was allowed to socialize with the seniors as a freshman, with all of the expected fringe benefits.

Anyway, back to Donnie: he gave me big hug. Donnie likes to hug; it's kind of creepy on the job, but what the hell, it couldn't hurt my status. Donnie was the shopkeeper at the Woods bus yard next door: that meant he had control of the bus parts, and other stuff as well.

Donnie asked me if I would like to see his shop. I said sure, things were slowing down at the party anyway. So we went down the stairs and through some parking lots, past a lot of buses. I thought it was odd that the men counting the money from the fare containers had the trunks of their cars open, but whatever, what do I know, I'm new. I read a couple of weeks later that the fair box department was all hauled off to jail for stealing. By the time I got back all the tables were put away, the people were gone, and Jimmy Lee was bright purple. Jimmy walked quickly over to me and placed his face not an inch from mine. He began his tirade with a splash of smelly saliva and some Mandarin. I couldn't make out what he was saying, but Bob and Von had to lead him away before he lost his temper even more, I guess. Jimmy, I found out later, believed I was hiding so I would not have to clean up from the party. I changed out of my work clothes and went home at the regular time.

Chapter Four

Streetcar Number 1

I was told to report to Metro the next day. Metro was the name of the Muni yard next to the Balboa BART station on San Jose and Geneva Avenue. It was a huge, bustling workplace, with trains, buses, trucks and shop vehicles roaring in and out 24/7. As I walked into the shop area, the first thing to hit me was the overwhelming smell of alcohol. Was the whole city work force drunk? How could a building five hundred feet long and two-hundred feet wide, with a thousand workers, open on all sides, smell like booze? But it did; this place smelled like someone had poured whiskey all over the floor. I went to the office that seemed to be the epicenter of the odor.

A nice man greeted me. "Can I help you," he asked. "Yes, I am from Woods. I have come to work on the historic Streetcar Number 1." "Oh yeah, you're Adam's helper. C'mon. I'll show you where the car is." We walked through hundreds of men, mostly machinists, working on huge machines. There were sheet metal men, glazers, and mechanics. Quite impressive, I thought, for all these people to churn out this much work while they are drunk.

When I looked upon this wreck of a vehicle, I immediately thought, how am I going to fix this? Just then, a familiar voice brought a smile to my face. Adam the Black Smith swung out from the back landing of the cable car and greeted me warmly. "We better get started, Laud." Adam had a funny way of saying my name. But I didn't care. I liked Adam. I guess Bob sent me here for the good of the shop.

The inside of Streetcar Number 1 was worse than the outside. All the windows were rotten; the floor was rotting. Half the seats were taken out and stacked in one corner. It must have been a lovely car at one time; it was fifty feet long and ten feet wide, shaped like a huge bullet. Adam the Black Smith showed me around. I had a little bit of a hangover from the scotch I had at Jerry and Johnny's, a bar downtown, the night before. I had been working a job in the evenings the last couple of months, trying to save some money for a new car. I would stop by Jerry and Johnny's on my way to the bus stop at about midnight. I'd have a couple of whips with a nice old guy tending bar. Howard was his name.

Adam and I worked hard on this car. We replaced the floor, both joists and plywood. We built new wood windows and trimmed the inside out with cherry wood. Jimmy Lee even got into the act. We never spoke of the party incident but I heard he quit drinking shortly after. The shop was making some of our trim. Shaping and planing the raw cherry wood was difficult. Jimmy was just the man for the job. This car was like a giant piece of fine furniture. Jimmy brought out some pieces and was quite taken back by the progress Adam and I were making. Jimmy started to take an interest in the project and we started getting along. I started to like Jimmy. I thought he was a decent guy with a family, trying his hand in a new country. I respected Jimmy when he was sober.

Before you knew it, Adam and I were putting the finishing touches on old Number 1. One warm afternoon one of the bosses came over to see the new car, a nice old guy about fifty years old. He smelled of alcohol but did not seem drunk. He complimented us on our work. The next day I heard that guy died in his sleep. Adam and I would work hard all day; at lunch Adam would tell me about Jesus.

I was sweating away, fine-tuning some of the new windows, when I felt someone enter the car. A handsome grey-haired man with a muscular build walked slowly over to my work area. We had been drawing a crowd the last couple of weeks. People seemed to be genuinely excited about this car. The good-looking grey-haired man walked slowly up to where I was working. I stopped and stood up. He looked around and felt some of the trim and scanned the almost finished masterpiece. "You know, people here don't care if you do a good job or if you're honest and hard working. They care how well you can drink, steal, lie and cheat." The guy paused and smiled. "My name is Dylon. I'm a painter." There was not a drop of paint on the clean, pressed blue overalls Dylon the painter had on. Every painter I knew had paint on most all of their clothes. Dylon's hair was perfect. He looked almost like he had had it cut, blow dried and styled that morning. I said hi and asked him what he thought of the car. He liked it, he said, "But I guess I'll have to paint it after you're done." I heard Dylon got beaten up by a lady painter some years later.

Adam went out sick, so I finished the car. I did not see much of Adam after that job, which made me sad. One of my last days at Metro I happened to be working on the car later than usual. I walked to the bathroom and I noticed a young man with a coffee cup and a handful of timecards standing by the time clock. I nodded the way construction workers do when they walk by another man. The guy smiled at me. Later, I found out this was Maynord. As I got to know him, I learned that he had one duty and one duty only: that was to punch his ten or so fellow painters in and out every day. In exchange for this, Maynord was allowed to drink rum and coke all day, every day, and never touch a paintbrush or paint. Maynord was hired as a painter and received an annual salary of approximately $70,000.00 per year. And when I spoke to him he thought he was being taken advantage of.

Bob Johnson, the carpenter foreman at the cable car shop, presented me with a formal commendation for the work I did on Car Number 1 and I had my picture taken. I returned to the shop in Dog Patch only to find Von had gone and Chet Rooney had taken his place at the shop. Bob introduced me to Chet, who had three of his fingers on one hand cut off. Since the job with the cable cars was what the city called a temporary job, I had been checking with City Hall to see what number they were on. About three hundred people had applied for these carpenter positions. I was number fifty, Von was forty-seven, and Rooney was forty-eight. Von had gotten a permanent call at the School District and planned to make his probation there and then; Bob Johnson would open a position at the cable car shop and Von would come back. This did not sound right but I did not want to make waves. Chet Rooney was basically doing the same thing at the cable car shop, only his job was waiting for him at the Department of Public Works. Chet Rooney took a couple of weeks of sick time over the next two months. He told us the story about how he had gotten his fingers caught in some machine at work and cut the fingers to shreds. Rooney was a nice guy, as far as I could see. He left after a couple of months.

I rebuilt a cable car that was involved in some kind of accident and received another commendation from Bob. I had been there almost six months when I got the news that Jimmy Lee was to be awarded "Muni Man of the Month." I was happy for Jimmy. We all went to the Cable Car Barn on Mason Street for the ceremony. Jimmy received a plaque, some money and had his picture taken. Pretty good for a guy who finished number eighty on the carpenters' test, could not speak English, and was an alcoholic.

The next day I was told by Jim McMan, the pattern maker, that Jimmy was to fill the open spot at the cable car shop if he liked. I found this strange. After all, he was at least one hundred people lower than me, and I wanted and needed this job. Once the permanent spots were filled, they might not need the temps any longer. I went to the foreman Bob, and asked how this could be. Bob did not have much of an explanation for me, but he did quote some type of rule having to do with six months on the job. It caused Lenny a great deal of joy to see me passed over for Jimmy; even though I rarely saw the two speak.

Nevertheless, I worked away. I went to the bar with Bob on Thursdays, worked my other job at night, and was able to buy that new car. Rooney came back with two more fingers cut off. I suggested he change occupations; he did not find that funny. Chet Rooney ended up back at the Department of Public Works as the carpenter foreman with five fingers—total.

Dave Menna started the day after Chet Rooney left. I went to grammar school with Dave's brother Jack Menna. Although he was a few years older than me, I had fond memories of him. Well, kind of. He was my crossing guard captain and my Scout leader. He was a San Francisco cop now, and gained some notoriety when some hoodlums tried to carjack him while he was in a leg cast. He sent two of them to the hospital. Some years later I saw him on the news doing an impression of his K9 partner for the reporter. Jack Menna loved uniforms, bossing people around, and wasn't contrary to whacking you around if need be: a police department dream. Twenty years earlier, when I was nine or ten, a hooligan at Our Lady of Mercy Catholic Grammar School by the name of

Trey Lister coaxed me into calling Jack Menna "Big Head Jack." I felt honored that I was probably one of the first people patrolman Menna beat up.

My mentor Billy would speak often about another carpenter by the name of Chip Merricik. Billy spoke fondly of Merricik. Von and Bob Johnson did not like him and called him terrible names when he was not present, but were very nice to him in person. Chip Merricik was not allowed in the shop. I was told it was because of some materiel and equipment that turned up missing after his last visit. Bob felt it was time for me to meet Merricik.

The cable car barn was technically under Bob Johnson's watch, but there was only one carpenter there, so the day-to-day assignments were handled by Dan Lobo, another supervisor in charge of the mechanics who worked on the cable cars. I was given Chip's check and told to bring it to him at the cable car barn on Mason Street, between Jackson and Larkin. I found the barn easy enough, but when I got inside the round house I could not find Merricik. I went to the office and introduced myself to Dan Lobo and asked if Merricik was available. Dan was a friendly man, about forty years old, with slicked back hair and a huge belly. He was easy to smile and he gave me a sly grin when I asked for Merricik. Dan brought me back to the carpenter shop, turned, and returned to his office. I looked around for Chip and disturbed several men in blue overalls gambling and two more sleeping in some recliners. I asked if anyone knew where Merricik was. A moment of silence followed; I was quickly scanned. I had my carpenter overalls on and the Muni I.D. tag we were required to wear. A Latin looking man told me to "Check the truck." I asked, "What truck?" Another young man got up from the Poker game, grabbed his twenty dollars or so, and said, "Come with me."

I followed the cleanest worker I had seen since Dylon the painter over to a small wrecked Toyota pick-up with a camper shell on it. The blue gambler knocked on the tailgate door and yelled, "Hey, Merricik, someone here to see you." I heard a mumble from inside. My helper said, "Sorry, I guess he doesn't want to be bothered." I told the worker I had Merricik's paycheck. "Hey Merricik, he has your paycheck," the worker yelled. Just then the camper shell back door flew open. A foul odor filled the air. "Phew," said the worker. Merricik lay fully clothed across an assortment of tools and rags. He turned his head; his eyes squinted, and put out his hand. I handed him his check. I began to introduce myself and the door shut abruptly. The worker laughed and called out, "You are an asshole, Merricik." I silently agreed.

I got my two week lay off notice at the cable car shop the same day I got my permanent call from San Francisco General Hospital: the Department of Public Health. I called and made an appointment with a fellow by the name of Bernard Blake. I said my good byes, got a hug from Donnie Bones, and off I went to my interview.

Chapter Five

General Hospital

Dave Menna, my friend from the

cable car carpenter shop and number forty-nine on the carpenters' hiring list, interviewed before I did. He probably was drunk; he usually was. Bernard Blake interviewed me. We were alone in the carpenters' shop for an hour. Bernard did his best to ascertain if I had the experience necessary to perform the job at the hospital. I felt rather bad for him. He really knew very little about construction work. The carpenters came in and we all talked for about an hour. Turned out that one of the carpenters, Chester Billings, went to Saint Ignatius High School with my uncle Richard. And my uncle Joe worked at the hospital. Taking all these things into account, I started the next morning.

Not being off work or missing any time due to a lay off was very important. I am not sure why, but it had something to do with a "break in service." With that, another set of consequences kicked in. The carpenter shop at General Hospital was huge; the paint shop, electrical shop and plumbing shop were next door. We had a gigantic bathroom with four private stalls and as many urinals. We had a lock on the carpenter shop, which made this bathroom private, I was told. No one could use or would use our bathroom and Chester Billings was the enforcer on that issue. Chester was forty years old at the time, 6'5" tall, and he weighed well over three hundred pounds. Chester had a blue vein that started at the bridge of his nose and traveled down the bridge, across the round red tip, then blended in with another group of protruding veins on the sides of his huge nostrils.

Red was the boss. Red shook a lot; I thought he maybe had Parkinson's. I worked with him one day and he trembled so he could not hold a screw long enough to drive it. He sweated profusely, and he was extremely unfriendly: he did not talk or show any kind of emotion.

My first assignment was to build a cart to transport my tools and fasteners around the seventeen-acre property. I tried to improve on the thrice accepted design; this was met with a great deal of mistrust and suspicion. Since all three of their tool carts were exactly the same, I felt a more lightweight and agile cart could make getting around faster and more efficient. In the construction world that I knew, this kind of thinking was considered good and progressive. "On the outside," how any job other than a city job was referred to, any action, idea, procedure or change in the order a task was done that resulted in a speedier completion or better product was revered and held in high esteem. If a task was done more speedily with the same good result, it was always a good thing. This meant another task could be completed, thus making more money for the company. Really simple stuff, I thought. I was finding out rather quickly that this place, the city, was like that Marvel comic book world were Superman is unshaven and his cape is torn and he is bad instead of good. I believe they called it the parallel universe.

Shortly after I started at the hospital I got the news my wife and I were expecting our third baby. Billings was a nice enough guy. Maybe because of the family connection, he seemed to take me under his wing and show me the ropes, so to speak. The day I started he showed me the large wooden table and the spot where he ate lunch, where Red ate lunch, and where Neil ate lunch. He gave me a choice of the remaining two seats. I picked one. He then opened the drawer below his spot and pulled out a quart of vodka. Bill said, "We keep our bottles in this drawer and at 3:00 p.m. we meet here for a drink before we go home." He opened Red's drawer, then Neil's, and said, "We get our own jugs and don't bother the other guys. What do you drink?" Chester asked. I said, "Vodka." Chester said, "We got 7-Up over there. We get our work orders from Bernard; Red looks them over, takes the ones he wants, then I get them and take the ones I want. Then they go to Neil. He will pick which ones he wants, and you get the leftovers. We spend Monday and Tuesday fixing the doors, cabinets and equipment, the weekend stationary engineer's damage. The rest of the time we repair or complete the tasks the outside construction firms leave and then we have a day to help the hospital staff with small jobs like bulletin boards and blood pressure machines."

Well, this sounded crazy, but what happened next was even crazier. Bernard was leaving, going back to Kansas or something, and a man by the name of Ralph Hanley was taking his place. We were called to a big meeting; everyone in the building and grounds departments was told to meet at the carpenter shop: five painters, four plumbers, six electricians, a steamfitter, four gardeners, and the four of us at 10:00 a.m. on Tuesday. Now, Ralph Hanley was a funny little guy, about five feet tall. His head seemed to be small, even for that little body. His eyes were close together—too close—and he walked with a swagger like George Bush, you know, that bow-legged walk, like their testicles are so big they can't get their legs closed.

Well, Ralph started the meeting by introducing himself, and then explaining that this was "his ship, and he had set sail. If anybody didn't like it, they could row ashore." He was a nervous little guy, about forty-five years old. Billings told me he used to be the biggest drunk in the city, but found the cure recently and was very tough since then. He reminded me of Humphrey Bogart in the Caine Mutiny when he was talking on the stand regarding the ice cream and strawberries. Ralph Hanley was crazy all right—crazy like a fox. A few weeks later when I came to work, Red was on vacation, Chester and Neil were out as well, and a carpenter was in the shop from a construction firm called Tricon. He was using the equipment and hauling in lumber, making a big mess. This young man was on the phone a great deal. I went into Hanley's office to see what was happening and I was told by the office not to worry about it. I went back into the carpenters' shop. When the worker was finished I asked him what was going on. He said, "I thought you knew; we sometimes do work here for the city, and Ralph said we could use your shop." He asked me if he was bothering me. I said no, and went about my work.

I got to know this guy a little over the next couple of months. The carpenter from Tricon told me that his boss and Hanley had a real sweet deal going. The more work Hanley could get Tricon, the bigger kickback Hanley would get. It was starting to make sense now: all the time we spent fixing and cleaning up after the outside contractors, Hanley was getting rich on kickbacks. Ralph Hanley was not the only one getting rich at General Hospital; many of the tradespeople had their share of drama and corruption as well.

Johnny the painter had some kind of deal with the purchasing department where he had access to the stored furniture and equipment. Johnny and some others would come by the hospital on Saturday mornings, pick up a truckload of city property, bring it to the San Jose flea market, and sell it. The information Johnny gave me was that this had been going on for at least the past twenty years. Johnny had worked at the hospital for twenty-five years and inherited this scam from his boss, as these types of scams were usually passed down to the next generation. Chester Billings had a scam, and I'm sure Neil and Red had a scam as well. I only got to know Chester's though: at one time, he was going to pass it on to me.

The carpenter that I took over for, Cal, had a client in the Mission with a building. A camera supply shop, or printing, or both—I am not sure. This building was maintained by Cal on city time with city tools and city materials. When Cal retired Chester got this job and it seemed that Billings wanted to pass it on to me. Chester brought me by there one afternoon in the city truck. We pulled up in front, plain as day, unloaded some 2x4's and some plywood we had gotten from the shop and brought it up to a storage area above the sales floor. Billings said we were going to build some walls here. We went to the cellar and he showed me some work to be done there. I nodded and told Billings I was pretty busy commuting and such, with the kids and so forth, and tried to back out. Chester said, "Think about it."

And then there was the "Jim Crow" bathroom scandal. I guess I was partly to blame for that. The carpenter shop had that huge bathroom that Billings liked to keep private. What I did not know about were Billings's racial politics. Chester Billings was a racist, and I mean, he hated black people. Renny, a friendly, intelligent electrician, asked me if he could use our bathroom. I said sure, unlocked the shop, and let him in. I went about my business. Before Renny could get out of the shop Chester returned. Chester Billings saw Renny leaving; Billings gave him a hateful look and Renny returned the favor. When Renny had cleared the shop, Chester asked me,

"What's that fucking nigger doing in the shop?" I said the man needed to use the bathroom. Chester Billings told me that I was never to let that "black bastard" in this shop again. Billings said, "I don't want to put my ass where that fucking nigger put his." This type of thinking turns my stomach.

I said, "Whatever your beliefs are, Billings, they are yours. This is a city bathroom. He is a city employee. He has as much business in that bathroom as you or me." Chester huffed and puffed then went in the bathroom and started cleaning. I thought this was hilarious and I said to Chester, "You don't want to use the same toilet, but you will clean up after him." That was the end of my mentoring from Chester Billings.

The bathroom issue did not stop there. Renny tried several more times to use the toilet in the carpenter shop. Billings had stepped up his involvement in the exclusivity of personnel who were allowed in the bathroom, so Renny went to Hanley. Apparently Hanley was closer to Chester's thinking, so a bathroom down the hall was built for Renny. This started another issue when Renny went to the newspaper regarding the Jim Crow Toilet. Hanley and the crooked administrator called a meeting. We were all chastised for being insensitive to people's color, and Billings's beloved bathroom was now open to all building and grounds personnel. A person would have a hard time keeping up with all the side deals and scams that were going on at San Francisco General Hospital.

This was 1987 and the AIDS crisis was in full bloom. The worn out bodies and sad faces were roaming the halls and grounds of the hospital. Even with this huge crew, the place was a rundown mess. The money was being poured into the upkeep and improvements only to be siphoned off by Hanley and his cronies before it could do any good. As usual, I was given the jobs that Red opted out of. Billings only took work for and around his friends, or people he thought were his friends. Chester would brag about the parties and dinners he was invited to with higher-ups in the system, famous doctors, and administrators. I believe he made most of that up. Neil had a girlfriend at the General Hospital, so he liked to work near her. More times than not my jobs were in the locked jail ward or the psycho floor, and many times the AIDS' ward. This was 1986 and 1987. The general public was not sure how you got the HIV virus exactly. This ignorance created quite a stir when we were asked to work on that ward.

Apparently, Billings, Neil and Red were on some type of unofficial strike against the AIDS' ward. The work requests had stacked up before I got there. This act of defiance had to do with some stand off between the nursing staff on the AIDS' ward and the maintenance department's feelings about safety. The nursing staff felt the patients would be humiliated and embarrassed if the carpenters were to wear the full hazardous waste outfits Chester and the gang felt they needed to employ while working in the AIDS' ward. This included a respirator, full jump suit, booties, gloves, and a hat. I had kept up on the AIDS crisis and gained some respect for the men: hollowed out humans with oxygen tanks roaming the site. A kid from my neighborhood, Terry Lane, was in the ward. I went to see him one night after work, but he had already passed. The word got around to the carpenter shop soon after my visit to find Terry and I was quickly given the assignment to install six blood pressure machines on the left side of six beds in the AIDS ward at San Francisco General Hospital.

When I received the work orders that morning, my jump suit was laid out for me with a respirator, hair net, gloves and booties. Chester Billings and Neil, with Red nodding in the background, angrily instructed me on the dangers of unprotected work in the AIDS' ward. They said, "Think of your family, man! You don't want to bring that dirty disease home to them, do you?" I did something that day I regret even now; I knew you couldn't get AIDS from working near AIDS patients. I knew it was wrong to follow these pigs. But I put the suit on; they nodded in unison as I pushed my fast, efficient cart towards the elevator. I saw my reflection in the elevator doors: what a fool I looked like. When I reached the ward, the wide doors opened when they sensed me. As I passed the nurses' station the attractive R.N. I spoke with a week earlier looked down. When I reached the first room on the work order, I knocked, and then entered. Both beds were empty, freshly made, with the curtains open and the spring sunshine shining through into the empty space. Terry's room, I thought.

I fastened the blood pressure machines, swept up the plaster mess I had made, and moved to the second room location. I wasn't as lucky here: both beds were taken. On my left was a young man sleeping; to my right was another man, sitting on the side of the bed. A nurse was helping him get dressed. As I entered the nurse flashed me a look I can still remember. She narrowed her eyes and asked me, "Do you really need to wear that?"

I said, "Yes, I do." The man getting dressed said, "Oh, leave him alone. He's trying to do his job." He smiled at me. I smiled back. The patient getting dressed was younger than me; he looked about eighteen, without even a full beard. He got up with the help of the nurse and was unsteady as he tried to stand straight. "I'm going home today," he said to me. The nurse held his arm and they walked slowly out the door. The door shut behind them and it grew very quiet in the room. I could hear the labored breathing of the sleeping patient behind me as I installed the machine.

I swept up my mess and turned towards the patient. He was awake now; he had put on an oxygen mask, which covered his nose and mouth. As I walked towards him I saw his large, saucer-like brown eyes. He had black hair. This kid didn't look even as old as the other guy; his emaciated body barely made a lump in the blankets. As I got closer his eyes followed me. He raised his eyebrows and his left hand made a slight gesture. He stared at me and I stared at him. His skeleton-like hand was holding the mask to his face. I suddenly felt hot; I turned and faced the dirty, crummy window. Bright spring sun was shooting through. I saw my reflection in the grimy glass.

I was having a hard time breathing; I ripped off the silly hat and tore at the respirator. I ripped off the gloves and booties and tore the paper jumpsuit off. I wiped the sweat from my face and neck with the wad of protective gear. There was a wastebasket against the wall. I shoved the ball of gear through the stainless steel swinging door. I turned towards the young man in the bed. A blank, empty stare followed me to my tool cart. I attached the blood pressure apparatus under the surveillance of the dark haired kid. We were alone in the room and he watched my every move. I was relaxed and calm and worked not far from his head. I finished my work and swept up. I turned to leave and I heard a faint "Thank you." I looked towards the young man; his mask was off and he was smiling at me—a big smile—his face was all smiles. I walked over to him. He held his hand up slightly and I squeezed his outstretched palm. He moved his hand some and smiled. We looked at each other for a few seconds. I smiled back before I turned and left the room. I finished the last two blood pressure machines. Things were never the same for me at General Hospital after that day. And it was the very last time I submitted to pressure from my ignorant, drunken, hateful coworkers. And my troubles were just beginning.

I gathered as much information as I could and got my carpenter friend from Tricon to tell his story. I then wrote and delivered a letter outlining the scams, the project kickbacks, and Hanley's plan to eliminate all the city construction workers at the hospital and increase the outside contracts, thus increasing his kickbacks. I never heard back from the administrator in charge of construction. What I did hear was that Ralph Hanley was eliminating the electrical shop, the plumbing shop, the painters, and the carpenters.

Ralph Hanley approached me with a couple of his big, ugly henchman the morning after I delivered the letter to the administrator. I wasn't too alarmed. I had my hammer and sheetrock knife handy in case things got sporty. Ralph told me, "You better be looking for another job." I asked why, not knowing if he had heard from his business partner: the administrator. Ralph said that I had broken the rules. I asked, what specific rule had I broken? Ralph Hanley yelled, red in the face, "You have broken all of them." I told him I wasn't going anywhere; I have a family. Hanley stated, "Better find a place to transfer to: I have already eliminated your position." I checked this out with my former mentor, Chester Billings, and spoke to Neil and Red as well. Billings told me he had seen the budget and this was true. Hanley and the crooked administrator had completed the budget for the next year and, sure enough, one carpenter position was eliminated. Hanley's plan was to eliminate all twenty trades-people and replace us with outside vendors. This was bad news for me: I needed this job. But on the other hand, I had had enough of the corruption, the stealing, and the drinking. It was probably for the better.

Chapter Six
Sunol

I called about every two days.

Orlando at City Hall would giggle. "Nothing yet, Lloyd,"
Orlando would say. I told him about the situation at General Hospital and over a couple of months we became
friends. I would tell him the goings on at the hospital
and he would tell me the crazy stuff happening in his department; we would console each other. I had never seen
Orlando in person, but we became close. Things were
getting tense between Hanley and me. Ralph couldn't
seem to wait for my transfer, so he assigned a stationary
engineer to follow me around. I truly had sympathy for
this man. His name was Edward and he was new: serv-
ing his probation. Edward followed behind Hanley, when
he wasn't trailing me, and kept notes, I guess. He had a
clipboard. Edward was handsome: tall and blond. He was
married with some kids, but looked about twenty. When
I would stop and talk with a nurse or co-worker, I would

sense someone looking at me, and there would be Edward, hiding around the corner with his clipboard. I usually laughed and tried to ignore him. Other times I would say, "Good morning, Edward." Edward would pause, then answer with a sigh.

Finally, Orlando came through, "Lloyd, I got something for you." "All right, Orlando! Where am I going?" "Water Department, Lloyd." I thought that would be great, except Orlando said, "Oh shit, Lloyd, it's in Sunol." "Sunol?" I said. "Orlando, where the fuck is Sunol?" "Fuck if I know. Buddy, I'll get back to ya." I spent the rest of the day counseling Edward on the perils of becoming Ralph Hanley's bitch and how that could affect his career and all. Edward looked very pained throughout the conversation.

Orlando called that afternoon. "Lloyd! Sunol is in the East Bay near Pleasanton. About an hour from the city; here's your contact." Orlando gave me a number and a name: Carl Essex, Plumbing Supervisor One. I called Carl that afternoon. Billie answered, and I called her "Sir." She corrected me with her low, scratchy voice. Off on the wrong foot they call it. I had an appointment the very next day. It was easy to transfer, if you could get another department to take you. They signed Orlando's form, and then my current department simply had to let me go. I stopped by City Hall the next morning, and met Orlando in person for the first time. He was gay.

I got the form from Orlando and drove over the Oakland Bay Bridge. I went southeast towards Pleasanton and Dublin. I passed San Ramon and took the Sunol exit. I came to this quaint little town with a post office and a pub. I drove past a huge lumberyard that said San Francisco Water Department on the iron gate. I came to a long, tree-lined driveway with a mansion-like building on one side. The shop area was in the middle of farmland planted with some kind of vegetables. There were some farmers working in the fields, but very little activity otherwise.

I pulled up to an office building with marked parking and a dozen city vehicles in front. I walked up the long walkway and entered a clean and organized office. Billie sat in front with the June sun shining brightly through the windows. It was only 9 a.m. in the morning, but it was already eighty degrees. I had a seat until she got off the phone. I knew it was her because her voice was more like a man's than a woman's. Billie was about eighty years old, and she looked every day of it. When Billie finished her call, a fifteen-minute call with a lot of laughing and whispering, I stood up and introduced myself. Billie said, "Carl is out right now, but he will be back shortly." She offered me coffee and I accepted. I waited in the hot, stuffy office for about fifteen minutes. Then I told Billie I was going outside for a breath of fresh air. Outside was hot: the mid-morning sun was strong. Sprinklers were on in the fields and the sun was low; a rainbow was shining in the distance. I felt good about this place.

A large pick-up pulled up in a cloud of dust. I stepped out of the way and greeted a tall gentleman. The man in the truck said his name was Carl Essex. Carl said, "You must be Lloyd," shook my hand, and gave me a big smile.

We went into Carl's office. He had a huge, air-conditioned space with a massive oak desk, a wall of windows, and framed pictures of construction workers on custom built-in shelving. Carl offered me a seat and asked me if I would like anything to drink. I said I would love something cool, so he asked Billie what they had. She went to a fridge in another room and brought out a Coke, a 7-Up, and water. I took the 7-Up and thanked her. She gave me a polite smile and left the room. Carl stood up and closed the door. I noticed he and Billie had exchanged a private look.

I thought what a large man Carl Essex was: tall, with a bald head, huge arms, and a grey mustache. He had on new blue jeans and a golf shirt. Carl slowly sat down, "So why do you want to work here," he asked. I told him it was the only job available, and General Hospital was eliminating my position. Carl laughed out loud. "Sounds like a good reason to me," Carl said. "Let me show you around, Lloyd." Carl and I strolled the grounds. We met Monty, a mechanic, and Shakes, a painter. We hurried a bit, so I didn't get a really good look at either one. We then got in Carl's truck: he wanted to show me the water temple. It was down a long, straight, road about a mile from the office. Once we arrived, we got out of the truck. Carl seemed like he wanted to tell me something. He looked down, shuffled his huge feet, and looked at me. "It's like this, Lloyd," Carl stuttered, "There is this guy that has worked here as a laborer for a long time. His name is Billy Bendesian. He took the carpenters' test, then got hired at the Water Department City Yard. I got the carpenter here to stay till Billy was hired somewhere else. And now he wants to come back to work here," Carl carefully explained. "I don't want him here," Carl said with conviction.

Well, I thought, don't that beat all: every move the city makes is based on some side deal or scam. I was only interviewed for the cable car shop so Ms. Brown could scare me away. I only got the job at the hospital because they didn't want John the alcoholic; the only reason John got the job at the Water Department was so Ben Bristol the foreman could torture him because John's brother, Ed, beat Ben up at the loading docks some years earlier. And the only reason I was going to be saved a lay-off was to fuck poor Billy Bendesian out of a job that probably should have been his. I took the job and started the next day.

I arrived at the Sunol maintenance yard at around 8:00 a.m. I quickly found out Carl Essex was a stickler for punctuality. After Essex berated a co-worker for being late, we walked around the yard. Carl introduced me to Monty, the mechanic, a nice gentleman about sixty years old with a huge scar down one side of his neck. We then met Casey: Monty's assistant, but everybody called Monty his Daddy. We met a guy by the name of Jack. He looked like my grandfather, with a huge belly and wide shoulders. He seemed unfriendly and indifferent to Essex. We then met Shakes, the painter, who was asleep in his paint shop, which did not seem to bother Essex. Shakes seemed embarrassed though and stunk like booze. Carl brought me to the carpenters' shop and then had to go.

I looked around at my shop. It was lovely and big, probably 1200 square feet. It was bigger than my house in Petaluma. Most of the tools were gone, just the outlines on the walls. I swept up and opened the windows to let the place air out some. Just then I heard a loud voice and a big red-haired kid came strolling in. He introduced himself as Baggs. He plopped himself into the wheelbarrow by the work bench and asked how did I like it so far. I said it seemed pretty good to me. Baggs was a good-looking guy, about twenty-five, I guessed. He was tall, about 6'2" or so, and laughed and smiled a lot. I liked Baggs right away. "Milton Baggs," he said, "I live in Hayward but I am from the city. Where you from?" Milton asked in a volume ten voice. I said that I live in Petaluma but I was born in San Francisco. "All right," Milton said. Milton Baggs got up out of the wheelbarrow and walked slowly out of the shop. As he got to the door he turned and winked, "See ya tomorrow." It was 11:30 a.m.

A steady stream of well-wishers came into the shop that day. Del Senior, the laborer foreman; his son Del Junior, another laborer who, as it turned out, was hoping to get the carpenter's job before I got there. He seemed a little bitter, but I let it go. Steve, Jose, Bill C., and Bill P., the other crew members, stopped by in the afternoon and welcomed me aboard, so to speak. Bill D. came in with Shakes the painter later on that day. Bill D. was the heavy equipment operator, although the two years I was there I never saw Shakes paint or Bill D. operate any heavy equipment. They mostly played the horses, drank vodka, and smoked weed.

The incident that sticks out the most in my recollection of the Sunol job is the lumberyard day. Carl Essex came out to the carpenters' shop a couple days after I started and told me I was to take inventory of the lumberyard in town and order what I needed for the next couple of months. This sounded great: I could get good lumber, maybe, not the shit the cable cars and the hospital had to use because of the kickbacks Ralph Hanley and Bob Johnson received to take the bad lumber. "Take Baggs with you, Lloyd," Essex hollered as he was leaving. I looked around for my large, red-haired friend and found him in the mechanics' shop sharing some laughs and what appeared to be an adult beverage the way everybody shook and hid their cups when I rounded the corner.

"Essex wants you to come with me to the lumberyard, Milton." The group in the mechanics' shop shot a strange, nervous look around to each other as I turned. Baggs met me at the truck. "I am going to take my own car, Lloyd, and leave from the lumber-yard, so I will meet you there." Essex had given me a large ring of keys a couple of days earlier, and the lumberyard key was clearly marked. The yard was easy to find. The town of Sunol was a cute little enclave of a couple of antique stores, two bars, a post office, and of course, The City and County of San Francisco's Water Department Lumber Yard at Sunol.

When I arrived at the yard, Milton was already in. He had the forklift fired up and the locked warehouse doors open. I waved at Baggs and started to list the inventory. A few pieces of redwood 4x4's, some studs, a few 2x6's—but really, the place was almost empty. I motioned to Milton that I was done. He said he would lock up and I returned to the compound. I was organizing my list when Essex popped in and asked, "What do we have in the yard?" I showed Carl Essex my list and he looked perplexed. "Well, we better get some more 4x4's and such. I'll order this batch, Kid." A couple days later Essex came out and told me to find Baggs and go unload the lumber trucks at the yard in town. I met Milton Baggs there and, lo and behold, we had two trucks with trailers full of redwood 4x4's. We barely had enough room for all the lumber, but we were able to fit the thousand or so redwood fence posts. I thought to myself, I must have a lot of fences to build.

A week or so later I went to the lumberyard to pick up some lumber, and every single 4x4 was gone. The gate was locked. I had heard nothing about a break-in. I quickly drove back to Essex's office. The plumbing supervisor was on the phone. Hearty laughs gushed from Essex's office. When I heard Carl hang up, I stood and walked in. I got a frown from Billie. "The lumber's gone!" I stuttered. As the words left my mouth and the sly smirk on Carl Essex's face hit me in the stomach like a punch, I realized what a fool I am. "Don't worry about it, Kid," Essex proclaimed, and simply said, "We will get some more." I found out some time later that Jack, the other equipment operator, had given or sold the fence lumber to his friends the cattle ranchers, who leased property from the city. And that's how it went for a while. In the mornings, Jack, Shakes, Monty and Casey would mix instant coffee, hot water and vodka to get started. They didn't hide it and even asked me if I wanted one. God no! I thought, but I was more polite, and just said no thanks.

I was sent over to the Millbrae yard to help out the carpenters there for a while. Millbrae is a small, well-heeled part of the San Francisco peninsula near the airport. The S.F. Water Department has a maintenance yard off El Camino Real that primarily takes care of Crystal Springs reservoir. As it turned out, Donnie Jeter and Jerry Reynolds worked there. Donnie was the storekeeper and Jerry was a backhoe operator. Gerald Lufkin, another plumber, ran this show. Gerald was from Daly City and had some kids my age: one of his boys knew my younger brother Bart, and apparently his kids knew of me. When I met Gerald in the common area of the complex he had a bullhorn that he used to berate and insult his crew. There were about thirty people in a cafeteria-like room, waiting for their daily work orders. These they would receive from Gerald Lufkin via bullhorn with some description of their appearance, or work quality and punctuality. I happened to have on a pair of slip-on van surfer shoes that morning and these were brought to the attention of the crew, as well as my status as a fill-in and helper. After that, a plumber I had never seen before told Lufkin he would take me out to breakfast then show me around.

We went to breakfast for an hour, and then the plumber dropped me off at the storeroom. Donnie Bones, who was drinking beer already, told me this was a country club and I should work hard to get here. Now, this seemed to be true: the grounds were really nice, with palm trees everywhere; some old, turn of the century buildings scattered about; a new lab area, and really nice weather.

Everyone seemed kicked back and content. Donnie said he lived nearby with his wife and had a little kid too. I congratulated him, and of course he gave me a big hug.

My first assignment was to assist in the rather large remodel of one of these turn of the century buildings. When I got to the area I was introduced to Oscar, the carpenter assigned to the Millbrae yard. Oscar was a massive man with huge hands. There was something odd about Oscar though. Oscar's clothes were dirty and wrinkled; his work boots had holes in them, with duct tape in different places. Oscar looked like he was forty years old or so. We worked together that day. When we sat down for lunch Oscar had a tuna fish sandwich and a very ripe banana. A helper proclaimed that Oscar always had a tuna fish sandwich and a banana. Oscar did not mind this observation. He agreed and offered more insight into his habits.

Oscar said he had lived in the same house all his life and was very much a creature of habit. Something was also wrong about this assignment: Oscar seemed to be going exceptionally slow, almost tediously slow, the kind of slow that takes more energy to accomplish than going at regular speed. After the second or third day, Oscar finally shared the reason for this behavior. "Lufkin's trying to fire me," Oscar said, dropping tuna and bread crumbs on his dirty shirt. "I have had the union out here already and they think I go fast enough," spitting banana as he spoke excitedly. "They brought you over to show that I was too slow," he said matter of factly. "When you leave Lufkin's bringing the union back out and show them what you did." I looked Oscar over: his dirty clothes, his tattered boots, his nervous way. Oscar and I didn't do much the next couple of weeks until I was sent back to Sunol. Not much was said following my return to Sunol; things went back to normal.

An exciting job came up though, and I was told to meet with a big boss in the empty office next to Essex's. Mr. Jenner sat behind a huge desk. "Do you think you could rebuild some of these old bridges, Lloyd?" I told the nice old guy sure, I had worked on bridges before. My uncle had actually built them but I had helped. This gentleman asked if I could meet with the engineers on the project and come up with a plan to replace some of the framing, along with the deck and curbs. I said sure, it sounds exciting, and I was thanked. I never saw that man again. I did meet with the structural engineer assigned to the Hetch Hetchy bridges, though. We went over some blueprints and I was given a full crew, including truck drivers, equipment operators, and laborers. I ordered some large timbers and had them delivered out to this remote area of the watershed.

This was a pristine wilderness area, with bobcats, wild turkeys, beautiful waterfalls, cattle, and lo and behold, stacks and stacks of my 4x4's. I told the operator that these looked like our missing lumber. He said no, just a coincidence. I did not believe him. The bridge job went superbly. I met Devin, Jose, and Stephen on that job: all laborers. Devin was the fifth or sixth son of a Water Department boss who was kind to Essex after one of his divorces, so Devin was hired and coddled by Carl Essex.

Jose was from El Salvador, which he had left either because the Sandinistas were looking for him, or he had sex with his cousin—I could not get a clear answer from him—but I liked both guys.

Now Stephen was an interesting case. We became good friends right away. He was a huge Irish man from the Sunset District of San Francisco, and apparently had some past trouble with liquor. When we started the bridges he was not drinking. One year later an ambulance took him away because he was vomiting blood. Stephen started throwing away the lunch his wife would make him and buying three tall beers and a half pint of vodka for the workday. Stephen never appeared to be drunk, not even when the ambulance took him away. Stephen and I went on a few city field trips together. I met his current wife and learned a little about his life.

In the 70s and 80s Stephen owned a bar, a very popular bar called Noe's in the Noe Valley district of San Francisco. Stephen would recite poetry when he got drunk and women seemed to like him. Stephen was found having sex with one of his waitresses on the pool table after hours by wife number two and the bar was sold a short time after that. Stephen's brother I met as well; another giant, but he looked much healthier, I thought. I do not recall his name, but he was quite the mover and shaker in San Francisco politics. He was on the Golden Gate Bridge Board and president of the local Laborers' Union. Stephen had worked at the Park and Recreation Department, but was temporarily assigned to the Sunol yard. Stephen told me he was waiting for a gardener's job. I thought I might have seen him the other day on 9th Avenue and Irving Street with a bunch of city workers from the park, but I wasn't sure. I liked Stephen and I hope he is still reciting poetry and charming the ladies somewhere.

That bridge went so well they gave me three more. I was just finishing the last one when I was told by Essex that two big-wigs were looking for me at the carpenters' shop. I went into the shop and I was met by Ben and Sandy. Ben was the carpenter supervisor from the city yard water department and his boss was a manager of some sort. They wanted me to come to the city yard and work. They told me there would be more money and a lot of overtime pay. I told them I would think about it, but they were very arrogant and pushy. The two said that I would have to make my decision soon. I should have seen the signs, but I really wanted more money. We needed a bigger house for the five of us and I was trying to get that. So I said all right, I will go, when do I start? They said great, and I started at the city yard in the Bayview section of Third Street the next day.

Chapter Seven

The Mayor's Nephew

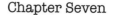

My first day at the city yard for the water department was pretty wild. This place was a huge operation,
with hundreds of men and trucks whizzing by the yard
and shop. A gigantic man by the name of Snake almost
ran me over with a big forklift as I was trying to make my
way to the carpenter shop. When I arrived, Ben looked
me over and went about his business. Ben Bristol was
a sour individual, about six and a half feet tall and very
badly dressed. I looked the men over and they did the
same. One by one they came by and introduced themselves to me on their own. First was Sammy Long, or
S.L., a young carpenter of small stature with psoriasis
all over his arms and head. Then a big Irishman removed
his face guard and earmuffs and revealed himself to be
my old friend, Dave Menna. We shook hands vigorously.
It was so good to see Dave, I felt like hugging him. The
rest of the crew looked on with curious amazement.

The next fellow was an old carpenter with a bald head by the name of Cass. Then came a twitchy, loud fellow by the name of Leonard Hickman. The shop was small and tense. Ben Bristol was a boring fellow with a beaten look. S.L. left in a hurry, slapping me on the back harder than was necessary as he exited. Hickman left right after S.L., talking to himself. Cass was working on an entertainment center made of oak and mahogany. He was not friendly—I had a bad feeling already. Bristol was giving Dave some orders and had not addressed me yet. Finally Ben said, "You go with Dave," and off we went in a newish green and white Ford S.F.W.D. pick-up truck. The first stop was a coffee shop on Monterey Boulevard. Dave ordered eggs and I got the same. Right after breakfast, Dave Menna vomited up his food. We got in the truck, leaving the mess behind. It was now 9:30 a.m. on my first day back in San Francisco. Not even two years into this city job it felt like twenty years already.

Dave and I arrived at our pump house right before lunch. We started sheet rocking the interior, and it was going well. A few minutes later, Ben showed up. "How's it going?" he asked. I said well, and he looked around and left. I mentioned to Dave that Ben seemed to ,be unfriendly.

Dave looked at me, paused, and said, "I'll say." For a couple of weeks that's how it went. I would get in the truck with Dave and we would eat breakfast. He would puke. Only we started stopping at Glen Park station for the two-thirty break. Dave would have two to three beers; I would have water, and we would go back to the shop.

Then Dave stopped coming to work and Bristol put me with Hickman.

Leonard Hickman was a piece of work: a stout guy, about forty years old, quick to laugh and quicker to steal. The first day I was with Leonard we shored a hole located in the San Francisco financial district. There was a pile of old cobblestones the backhoe operator had dug up. Leonard rudely ordered me to load them in the truck. I usually do not respond to that kind of rudeness, but I figured I was new, and I needed the job. We loaded one hundred or so cobblestones, shored the hole, with me doing most of the work, and headed back to the shop. We got on the freeway, but instead of returning to the Bayview, we headed for Daly City. I protested and told Hickman I needed to go home. He shouted some and told me to shut the fuck up.

We arrived at a run down house near the top of the hill in Daly City. Leonard ordered me to unload the stones. I said, "Unload them yourself—I am no thief." He said, "You want to get back to the shop, don't you?" "All right." We unloaded them and were back on the road in an hour or so. When we made it back to the shop it was a half hour past quitting time and Ben was livid. "Where the hell were you guys?" Ben shouted, leaning his six and a half foot frame over me. I was already tired of this sour ogre. I said, "Ask Hickman," and I changed my clothes and went home.

The next morning I was presented with a discipline sheet about returning to the shop late. I said, "Wait a second, Leonard was driving. I wanted to come back, but he had to go home." Ben said it didn't matter; we were both at fault. Hickman laughed and I told Leonard to go fuck himself. On our next assignment Leonard and I shored up a second hole and then another. I noticed I would always go in the hole, and then give the measurements to Leonard. He would cut the lumber and hand the pieces down to me. The man in the hole had the dangerous job for the simple reason that we were shoring the hole so men could work in it without it collapsing and burying someone; this was the most common way construction workers were killed. I thought we should rotate who went down into the hole and who stayed on top. Leonard Hickman disagreed. We argued, and I refused to go in the hole all the time. When the bosses showed up, I told them of our disagreement. The man that came to Sunol to lure me over to this hell ordered me back in the hole. I finished up that hole and the next morning Hickman was upset with me.

Hickman cornered me out in the yard and said, "Why don't I take you out of the gate and kick the shit out of you?" Now I had had just about enough of these empty threats from crazy city workers. I calmly told Hickman, "Let's not wait a minute longer. No one is around. Let's settle this right here and now. I fingered my claw hammer at my side, ready to bury the head in his thick skull. Lucky for Leonard, he came to his senses and walked away. I never had any trouble from Leonard Hickman after that day.

The next morning Dave Menna was back, looking really bad. As punishment Ben Bristol had Dave cut blocks for the plumbers every morning for an hour or so on the massive radial arm saw. Dave would cut 16 foot 2x6's into 12" pieces. Dave's hangovers looked painful. With the loud humming of the massive saw, the heavy boards, and the plumbers demanding more and more service, this certainly seemed like bad duty. And it was never rotated. One morning I helped Dave carry the boards, and we talked about Ben Bristol and his obvious anger and dislike of Dave Menna. Some years back Dave's older brother Bob was working as a longshoreman. Ben also worked on the docks, not as a longshoreman, but a clerk. Ben would count the broken and missing pallets, then report back to the bosses about who was responsible. Apparently Bob Menna had to correct Ben's behavior once or twice. So when Ben had the opportunity to get Dave back for Bob's actions, the coward Ben Bristol was, he took it out on Dave and made Dave's life at work miserable.

Ben was a bully: my first payday, Ben gave the checks out and when he came to me, there was no check. Ben Bristol didn't say a word—he just turned around and walked away. I walked up to Ben and asked politely, where was my check? Ben turned with that sour look on his face and said, "How the fuck should I know?" I calmly stated that he should fucking know because he was the fucking foreman and it was his responsibility to get me my fucking check. I was trying to figure out what I had done to Ben Bristol and why he was mad at me. My brothers never beat him up, although both of them could, probably my sister too. Then it dawned on me: Ben was a big shot in the union. I was a union foreman when I came to the city. Ben wasn't even a carpenter. Ben got the job through a friend. Believe it or not, 6'6" Ben Bristol was intimidated by me, even though he was my superior and twice my size. The troubles Ben Bristol had with longshoremen and carpenters became very clear. Ben Bristol is the world's biggest pussy: six foot six, 300 pounds of pure yellow coward. No wonder Ben got slapped around a lot. Finally after four weeks at the city yard some overtime came my way.

Overtime

Sammy Long and I were told to meet at this site on Turk Street after work. Sammy Long got ready to go about 3:00 p.m. He hollered for me around 3:30 p.m. Sammy Long, or S.L., as he was affectionately known at the yard, apparently was very popular, but only because his father was currently chief of police and his uncle was the mayor. I had an idea he was somewhat of an embarrassment though, or should have been. He was always either drunk or hung over. He was loud, abusive, and not very bright. I did not care for Sammy Long, but I guess like most people, I faked it. I wasn't sure if the father and uncle might work for me sometime. Fifteen years later we took the same test for supervisor. I placed a hundred people or so ahead of him. I remember he drove across town to yell something unkind at me from his water department truck, although I could not make it out.

The overtime scam at the San Francisco Water

department was simple, but lucrative. The overtime system was fairly easy to understand. I actually appreciated its simplicity and efficiency. Most plumbers worked as much overtime as they wanted, as long as they were in good standing with the shop steward, who also sold the coke, and the dozen or so bosses. But staying in good standing was not as simple. Now, the game was run like this: a water break would be reported, usually several a day. The man at the phone, a fellow named Mort, would alert the bosses. They would go out and look at it, but wouldn't write anything down yet. The foreman or boss would then start assembling his crew. At or around 3:00 p.m. the water break would be officially reported. The crews would finish their assigned work for that day, which was a water line break from the day before. Many men on their twentieth hour of paid overtime would get ready for some more. That's how plumbers, laborers, foremen, and bosses earned sometimes twice their base wages. But that's not even the sweetest part of the deal.

The night I went out to Turk Street, my first overtime, the golden palace was opening up for me, finally. I was excited. I was at the top of my game; I had been working as a carpenter for fifteen years. I had been a foreman, a superintendent, and a project manager. I was fit and had a lot of energy. I was thirty years old, with three children, a house mortgage, and money hungry as hell. We met at the job at 5:00 p.m. It was winter, so it was already getting dark. A large, handsome man came over and said, "There isn't anything for you guys right now, but stick around." I asked S.L. who that was. S.L. said that was

Jack: Captain Midnight. "Right on," I said. We waited and waited. S.L. took off for a while. I sat in the truck. Every once in a while I would get out and stretch, maybe talk to a flagman or plumber.

The water line fix was going very slowly. S.L. and I had done absolutely nothing so far except drink coffee and talk. Pretty soon it was around midnight; S.L. was still gone when the bosses showed up. The Captain came over to the truck and asked if I was alone. I said S.L. is around here somewhere. The nice looking boss with white hair and a tan face introduced himself to me as Jack. He told me he was running this show, and if I needed anything to let him know. I said okay, and we shook hands. Captain Midnight was about six feet tall, and kind of overweight. He had nice clothes though, so he looked good. He was checking with the plumbers and the backhoe operator. I watched him work from the window of my water department pick-up.

Just then, a late model, four-door luxury car swerved around the flagman, who was busy smoking a cigarette. The driver of the car seemed confused. The car careened inside the work area consisting of maybe ten trucks, parked at different angles, huge lights shining into a thirty foot long by six foot deep trench, and twenty men, mostly standing around, but some in the hole working. I thought: this could be bad. As the car headed towards me I started to exit my vehicle, almost instinctively, to either fight or flee. Just when it looked like the car was going to crash, Midnight jumped through the yelling and running workers and hale of coffee cups, onto the hood of the car.

He rolled over on his belly, looked the driver right in the face, asked him what the fuck he was doing, and then rolled off with the agility of an Olympic tumbler. The big car sped off into the crowded Tenderloin. I can't help but think that the Captain did this for me. I swear we made eye contact as he was dismounting.

According to Jack, the department boss, overtime was not as lucrative as the cocaine trade at the yard. Jack, or Captain Midnight, as I was told he liked to be called, said he would trade his overtime, which was substantial, maybe a thousand hours a year, for the cocaine business anytime. I laughed; he did not. Finally, at around 5:00 a.m. S.L. and I were on. A plumber came over and asked us to shore the hole. We did this in about forty-five minutes and we were told we could go. So, we were on site for twelve hours. We did forty-five minutes of work. I was curious to see how this worked. We went to breakfast and returned to the shop. We unloaded our tools and went home before the other workers came in. I went home and got some sleep.

That afternoon I was called to come back in and we worked that night till about 1:00 a.m. The next day was Friday. When I returned to the yard I was called to the office. Captain Midnight asked me how I liked it at the yard. I said I liked it fine, and that I came there for the overtime, so I was happy to get some these last few days. Midnight smiled and said, "Does twenty-four hours of overtime sound good for the work you did?" I said it sounded great. Now I thought that was for both nights, which was fairly close, but it turned out that was just for the twelve hours I sat at the Turk Street job, at time and one half. I was getting about twenty dollars an hour back then. It was nice: I took my family to the movies and out to dinner. Unfortunately, that was the last overtime I got at the city yard.

My relationship with Ben Bristol remained strained. I felt he was a bully and he abused my friend Dave Menna. And I would let him know. Dave drank a lot—and I mean a lot. Not too much at work; maybe a beer or two to "get well," like my friend Stephen from the Parks and Recreation Department, via the Sunol yard, via The Department of Public Works. Hard core drinkers like Stephen and Dave felt bad most of the time unless they had a certain blood alcohol level: an alcoholic didn't feel right, so "getting well" meant having a pop or two. Most of my bad relationships as a city worker were with alcoholics: many were paranoid and because of their disease, prone to dishonesty and theft. Now, I was not a policeman. I was not in charge of stealing or the stoppage of stealing, but because of their inherent paranoia, if I did not steal or drink a lot I always was looked on as a threat or a possible "snitch." I did not like being pressured into immoral behavior or dishonesty and I did not appreciate being distrusted.

Ben Bristol may have been an alcoholic. He certainly had the immoral behavior: he was a thief and he was distrustful. But most of all, he was a bully. He abused his authority and he was uneven with his wrath—which I didn't like either. Sometimes I thought: who the fuck am I to require this good behavior all the time, and

believe me, I wished I could stop. But I am just too careful who I spend my time with, and I did not like spending
it with the Chief of Police's coke-head son, the town bully,
and an assortment of thieves and liars. But I liked Dave
Menna.

Dave was an honorable man. Dave would always
do what he thought was right. Dave tried to control his
drinking, and had some success here and there while
we were friends, but mostly he was hung over or getting
drunk. When all is said and done, it would take a hundred
Ben Bristols to equal one Dave Menna, and at least that
many Sammy Longs, coke dealing shop stewards, or live
at home drunken drug addict white boys who only had
status because their fathers worked for the city before
them. I had had it with such a corrupt organization as
the water department. It must have shown through: I
was never one able to hide my feelings. Ben would have
Dave Menna cut blocks on the dangerous old radial arm
saw every morning for the plumbers. Ben would require
Dave, and only Dave, to perform this task. Oddly enough,
Ben Bristol did not give direct orders to the others, S.L.
and Q-Ball head Cass or Hickman. They wouldn't help a
crippled old lady unless money was involved.

I started to work with Dave when he struggled with
a bad hangover or just if he had a lot to do. This was
met with a great deal of scorn from my co-workers, which
couldn't have pleased me more. Finally six foot six inch
Ben Bristol stormed over to me one morning. He leaned
over, putting his large red face close to mine, and bel-
lowed that I had my work and Dave had his. Now if I had,

or if anyone else had, work to do first thing, I might have thought twice, but from 7:30 a.m. to 8:30 a.m. we didn't really do anything. Only Dave Menna was required to bust ass. And that was my answer to bully Ben Bristol. If Ben had a red face prior to hearing that bit of information, his face was a deep crimson afterwards. As usual, Bully Bristol backed down and stormed off. How could a guy that large have such small stones?

Speaking of stones, S.L., the Mayor's nephew, liked to antagonize certain individuals, people who were in a bind, people who had so much other stuff going on they could not retaliate. This quality I detest in a man, but it showed me Sammy Long was not a complete idiot. The first unfortunate soul I witnessed S.L. abuse was a man in the yard, whom I believe was a laborer or an individual who did labor. "Snake" was what S.L. called him. He would greet Snake with a loud "SNAAAAAKE" most mornings as the worker was going about his duties moving lumber with a gigantic forklift. Snake looked to be about forty, a little overweight, with a shaved head. Snake was brown but I never got close enough to him to really see if he was black or Latin or Italian. The worker S.L. referred to as Snake didn't seem to enjoy the nickname as much as S.L. and his cronies did. As far I could tell, he would have liked to run this little scaled coward right over with that huge forklift. I made sure I was far away from Sammy Long when he started to abuse Snake.

One morning my curiosity got the best of me and I inquired about the name and constant teasing of Snake. S.L. calmly stated that Snake had come to work one morning a few years back, suffered some type of psychotic break, ripped off all his clothes and run around the yard, begging his co-workers to get the snakes off him. Apparently Snake had stayed on his medicine or off it for some time and was very quiet and a hard worker. But of course, if you were brown, you had to watch your step in the yard. Sammy Long knew this and that is why he relentlessly tortured Snake and Dave Menna. Sammy Long enjoyed poking fun at my friend Dave Menna, which bothered me as well. It wasn't that Dave Menna couldn't take care of himself—Dave could have broke this little wise ass momma's boy in half—but Dave understood people's frailties. Dave Menna could see through the abusive and flamboyant behavior of young S.L. This was harder for me: shortly after I arrived at the city yard, S.L. called out for Dave Menna, using a favorite nickname. Since Dave had gotten a vasectomy, Sammy Long liked to call him "Davey Steer." I found this extremely ironic, largely because a steer is a male calf that has been castrated.

Dave Menna was extremely brave and honest, straightforward and kind, willing to stand up when things weren't right. Dave Menna knew Ben Bristol was hurt about being embarrassed by Dave's brother some twenty years ago. Dave Menna knew what a small man Ben Bristol really was. Dave knew S.L. was a weak, scared, incompetent carpenter riding on the coattails of a politically connected family. Yet Dave Menna did not resist Ben Bristol's abuse, nor did he squeeze little S.L.'s neck, which he most certainly could have. Dave took it because his abusers were weaker than him and it would be dishonorable to pick on a weaker man. Now that is what it means to be a man; that's what you could call balls.

I, on the other hand, was not as strong as Dave Menna. I detest bullies. I needed my job though, so I went about my business as subtly as I knew how. Nonetheless, I confronted Sammy Long on his Davey Steer remark one day when we were alone. I thought without his audience around, S.L. would not react out of embarrassment. I asked Sammy Long why he called Dave Menna, "Davey Steer." S.L. got extremely nervous and whispered lightly that, "Dave had got a vasectomy." I explained to S.L. that when you get a vasectomy they do not cut your balls off; they snip a tube that delivers sperm to your semen. I told S.L. that making that kind of joke would get his ass kicked if he were not dealing with a gentleman like Dave Menna. This really got S.L. nervous. I thought maybe he was going to cry. But instead, he stepped back from me and said, "You better not fuck with me." S.L. stated this very loudly and a few people in the yard stopped to listen. It looked like S.L. was very nervous and scared, even though I made no aggressive moves. I was smiling and very casual. S.L. started to walk away, repeating his warning in a matter of fact fashion, as if I should have known he was no one to fuck with. I calmly and quietly asked S.L. why I had better not fuck with him. This perplexed our nut-less yard comedian. I do not believe anyone had ever asked him that. Maybe he had gotten away with just stating, "You better not fuck with me." I started to chuckle a little. I did not want to be cruel; I just could not help it. After an uncomfortable amount of time Sammy Long said in a very quiet, high voice, "Because I'm crazy; that's why you better not fuck with me." I said okay. Actually, I thought we got along better after that day, but I was transferred back to Sunol a short time later.

When I got back to Sunol, not much had changed: Shakes the painter was still drunk in the paint shop, the other old-timers still drank vodka and instant coffee every morning, it was still hotter than Hades in the summer and freezing cold in the winter. Essex seemed overly pleased with himself that I had returned. This entire exercise could have been orchestrated by Carl Essex.

Chapter Eight

The Port of San Francisco

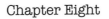

I started to feel resigned to the

fact that I might be at the Sunol yard for the rest of my career. My wife and I had bought that bigger house in Petaluma we needed for the expanding family. I was getting used to the shenanigans at the water department. I thought if I could buy a house in nearby Pleasanton, Livermore, or even Tracy, our situation might be better. I would be close enough to come home for lunch, the schools were pretty good, and I was starting to enjoy the country feel of the Sunol yard. We started to shop for a house in Pleasanton. It didn't take long before we found out the prices were just too high. This was 1988 and the price boom for California Bay Area real estate was in full bloom. Houses were going up in value at a rate of fifteen to twenty percent a year. So was my house in Sonoma County. Although I had bought my mansion for $140,000, in two years it had doubled in value. I was feeling pretty good about myself and mortgage lenders were beating down the door to lend us money on this new found $140,000 in home equity. But we kept our heads and were looking to "buy up" in Alameda County. We even found a Livermore house we liked, near good schools and in our price range. We put in our offer but they countered out of our price range. We decided to put the move on hold and see how Sunol went.

I took the City and County of San Francisco building inspectors' test and did pretty well. One of the proctors thought I might have been the youngest man ever to take the test. This didn't surprise me: the city wanted ten years of journey level experience in a major trade like carpentry, plumbing, electrical, and so forth. Then you had to have four years as a supervisor of a major trade. This was hard to acquire legitimately before the age of thirty-five unless you started at fifteen like I did. I found out later that they threw part of that test out because some of the applicants couldn't read the blueprint section. I thought they had purposely left out some of the measurements in order to prompt closer examination of the corresponding dimensions. This is the condition of some building plans; details that can be estimated, such as a closet dimension or bathroom size, are left out. Little things like this I thought would give the tester some insight into whether the test taker had actually supervised building before. Alas, that part of the test was removed; my strongest talent and I ended up with a seventy-four. I was told by the nice fellow at the human resources office I could appeal, but that usually creates some distrust of the appellant.

I thought it would be more prudent to bask in the fact I had qualified to take the test before I was thirty years old—possibly a record—and also the knowledge that I would have done very well had the blueprint section not been removed. My plan was that I would take it again at some point.

My old friend Keiren O'Reily called me one night and informed me that his father, William O'Reily, at the Port of San Francisco, had heard about my bridge building at the Water Department as well as my bad luck on the building inspectors' test. William O'Reily, through his son Keiren, wanted me to come to the Port and speak to Cam Stoutman, the carpenter foreman. Cam Stoutman was a tall man, close to a foot taller than me. A tired look hung on his face, like every bottle of whiskey he had drunk. Cam might have been a good-looking man at some point, but he was a worn out fellow now. The skin of his face was loose and wrinkled; he had a sad smile that made his watery eyes droop; and his massive eyebrows covered his lids. He smoked those little cigars and was quick to laugh, not a normal laugh, but a resigned, oh well kind of guffaw. "So where are you from?" he asked, bending over as we walked through the shop area. "I've been at the Water Department," I said, "For two years."

The first guy I met was Guadalupe Guadalupe. That's right, two first names. Guadalupe was a friendly fellow. He was the shop man; that means he did all the cabinet work. Guadalupe told me he was a pattern maker for the Navy in his native Philippines. Guadalupe said he looked Chinese, he had a Latin name, and spoke Tagalog:

a typical Philippino. The second person I met was Danny Jamali, a young man with braces on his teeth. He looked as if he worked out with weights: he was only about five feet tall, but he was built powerfully and weighed about 200 pounds. He slicked his jet black hair straight back, then pulled it forward in a pompadour style. Cam Stoutman was showing me around the shop. I had been there before when I took my carpenters' test in 1984. I mentioned this to Cam; I think he ignored it.

We entered the break room and locker room, which doubled as the kitchen. The light was off when we entered. As the door opened, a strong aroma of alcohol and body odor filled the air. I heard some profanity growled. Cam Stoutman quickly shut the door. Guadalupe and Danny chuckled. Cam Stoutman said, "That was Barry. You will find out about him soon enough. We got one other carpenter and a pileman who works out of the shop, but they are out in the field."

Cam Stoutman told me I had the job, and to "Go do my paper work." I knew what this meant. I had gone through the paper work now three times earlier: once when I started with the city in 1986, again when I went to General Hospital, and lastly for the water department. So, I was an old hand. I went to retirement. I went next door to health services. I went to General Hospital to get a physical. I didn't get done till after 4:00 p.m. Quitting time was four o'clock at the Port, so I went home to Petaluma feeling pretty good. I considered this could be a good fit; Stoutman seemed like a decent guy, Guadalupe and Danny were friendly enough, and I did not give the sleeping giant, Barry, too much thought.

I returned the next morning at 7:00 a.m. Starting time was not till 7:30 a.m. I greeted the men in the front glass-walled office with a construction worker nod, and walked slowly to the carpenter shop. The shop was open, but no one seemed to be around. I took the opportunity to familiarize myself with my new surroundings. Wow, I thought, a lot of equipment. As much as the cable car shop—way more tools and machinery than I had at the water department. I then walked into the locker room. Before I could switch the light on, I noticed the same lump on one of the benches.

Suddenly, a stack of wrinkled and unwashed denim unfolded itself from the wooden bench. In one fluid movement he reached for the door and slid by me as I stepped aside. A terrible odor wafted around me as he passed. I swung around and watched as he swerved towards the hallway and disappeared, mumbling, down the long hallway of Pier 46B. I was so enthralled by this act I did not notice the full shop to my left: Guadalupe and Danny were giggling to each other; an older, white haired fellow I had not met was shaking his head. Cam Stoutman and a huge, younger man with massive arms and a barrel chest were trying to ignore the bench warmer's exit, but still looked embarrassed as I shot them a puzzled look. Cam Stoutman invited me over to meet the rest of the crew.

The first to offer his hand was Kimball, a pileman who looked to be seventy years old. Kimball seemed like a real nice guy. The next up was Kerry. Kerry Greene had a mouthful of chewing tobacco. He looked to be well over six feet tall and at least three hundred pounds. His whole body shook when he laughed, and he laughed all the time. The smelly guy wandered back into the shop as I was waiting for my assignment for the day. He was a tall, athletically built man with greasy dark hair, a mustache, and a week's growth of black beard. He shot me an angry look as he got into a brand new Port of San Francisco truck and drove off without a word. Once again, Guadalupe and Danny laughed quietly; Kerry and Cam Stoutman looked embarrassed; and Kimball, the pileman, shook his head in disgust. I guess Stoutman noticed my puzzled look, so he told me that was Barry, and he was going through a divorce. Cam showed me a locker in Barry's quiet room, and told me to ride with Kerry and Kimball: he would meet us at the wharf. I said great, pulled my carpenters' overalls on, grabbed my toolbox, and threw it in Kimball's and Kerry's old pick-up. Again, this got Danny and Guadalupe giggling. I started to think I had made a mistake coming to work here; things seemed a little crazy and this locker room smelled horrible.

Pile Butts

The huge blond kid and Kimball Longstreet, the white haired gentleman, hopped in the truck first. Kerry started the engine with a puff of white smoke and a spit of tobacco. We were off, out of the Pier; exactly where Pac Bell Park is now, home of the San Francisco Giants. We drove rather fast down the Embarcadero, under the old freeway, past the dilapidated ferry building, whizzing by prostitutes and homeless people until we reached Fisherman's Wharf. It was a sunny San Francisco morning, rather cold, but bright. Kerry pulled up behind a group of similar Port vehicles, shot Kimball a knowing look, and quickly jumped out of the tall pick-up. This big guy could sure get around, I thought. Kimball was the opposite: he could not get around. Kimball was old—I mean really old—his gait was uneven, so it always looked like he was stumbling as he walked. I might have looked at Kimball too long: he shot me a hateful stare as I met his eyes. I quickly looked away. Cam Stoutman drove up next, as the three of us walked along the Wharf in our carpenters' overalls. Cam had another man in his truck. Now this guy looked like he might have been eighty years old. They were both clutching large coffee cups and laughing out loud. Cam joined our promenade as we made our way to the seafarers' chapel near a fish processing plant. We all stared at some rotten decking. A few comments were made regarding past experiences, and off we went back to the truck. As we made our way along the wooden pier, I could not help thinking back to when I was in high school.

We had a field trip to Fisherman's Wharf in my History of San Francisco class. I loved a girl in that class: Jenny Baron was her name, and boy did I have it bad for her. Jenny was the high school girl who really didn't look like a high school girl—you know the ones. She was 5'8"; with long black hair; an Irish complexion, clear and white; lovely brown eyes; and her body is what high school juniors dream about. I sat with her and had lunch, with three other boys thinking the same thing I was. I really did love Jenny Baron: I wrote songs to her, I brought her flowers, I took her out, kind of, a couple of times, but I don't think she ever looked at me like I looked at her. One stalling point could have been I never touched her, not even her hand or shoulder. I was terrified of her, I think. She was always kind to me, though.

Suddenly a loud voice broke the morning silence, "Where the fuck were you yesterday?" I turned, stunned, to face the outburst: Cam Stoutman, the white haired man, and the giant stood still with mischievous smiles. The old guy in Cam Stoutman's truck quickly rolled down his window and craned his neck. I jerked my head back to the voice and observed a group of men, all white bearded, all clad in Carhardt overalls with union logos on their jackets. The four workers laughed among themselves and the accuser spoke again, "Where the fuck were you yesterday?" This guy was the smallest of the group. He was about my size, but at least fifteen years older. I looked at my group a second time, hoping for some guidance. Cam Stoutman, Kerry Greene, and Kimball Longstreet all stared at the ground this time. No help there, I thought. I scanned the area fast: two more Port vehicles were parked nearby, so more Port workers, I thought.

"None of your fucking business," I answered, as I walked over with the half smile of a man who might pop you in the kisser. The curious show-off looked to the ground and I turned and joined my truck mates. We walked in silence to the truck. Cam Stoutman left quickly, without a word. His old, blue faced running partner next to him froze in thought. We got to Kerry's truck and Kimball Longstreet went to the back tool chest, fished around a bit, and pulled out his jacket: a Carhardt with the same union label: "Pileman's Union." Hmmm. I asked Kerry who that was. Kerry smiled big with tobacco stained teeth, "That is our new boss." Fuck, I thought, here we go, another Ben Fucking Bristol, another Hickman, Good Lord.

We all went for coffee at Red's Java House. As I walked in, the place was filled with Port workers and, sure enough, there sat four of the pilemen from this morning's go-round. They gave me a nod and spoke to Kimball and Kerry directly; we ordered our coffee and sat down. The first to come over was a handsome fellow around my age. He thrust his large palm my way. "How you doing, Cory's my name." I shook his hand and introduced myself. The next guy over was named Jerome. I had never really seen a fellow like Jerome before. He was rather short, but must have weighed three hundred and fifty pounds. He had a full head of hair and a perfectly trimmed Abe Lincoln kind of beard. He looked and sounded like he might have been retarded. The next up was Ronnie. He was about 6'2", and smelled like booze. His clothes were dirty but he was quick to smile and I liked him right off. Then came Chuck Welton, the foreman or lead man of some sort, I guessed. Chuck Welton was a nervous, large, dangerous looking man with bloodshot eyes and liquor on his breath: not old liquor, but like he might have had a beer and a shot just then. It was 9:00 a.m. Chuck made some comment on my short conversation with curious George earlier on the Wharf. Cory shook his head at Welton. The retarded Abe Lincoln look-a-like and Ronnie stared at the ground as Chuck looked me over. I did not like Chuck Welton and Chuck Welton did not like me.

Chapter Nine

Big Daddy

Kerry, Kimball, and I returned

to Pier 46B, the Port of San Francisco's maintenance yard and shop, a bustling enterprise with engine mechanics, machinists, heavy equipment operators, sheet metal men, electricians, painters, plumbers, iron workers, welders, roofers, construction divers and, of course, pile butts. Pile butts and pilemen are the same thing: they called themselves pile butts and they also did the diving. There were truck drivers and laborers—a lot of laborers. And when I say enterprise, I mean enterprise: it was mostly Big Daddy's enterprise.

Jack Hornbeck ran the Port of San Francisco's maintenance department. Officially, Cap was the boss. He sat in a trailer near the water at the entrance to 46B. Cap had a full-time secretary, another old, white-haired lady, usually a young person doing some kind of internship, and of course the trouble desk. The trouble desk was a rotational position used for various reasons. My first year there was a man by the name of Bob Jr.: he was a pile butt who had gotten hurt on the job. The Port had its own rules. Workers were suspended, hired, fired, laid off, promoted, kicked, beaten up, made to quit, threatened, shunned, and reassigned without any official city paperwork. The trouble desk took calls for emergency repairs. Depending on the qualifications of the person at the desk, you could fill out work orders, plan maintenance, troubleshoot the problem, meet with the client, take a bribe, deliver a bribe, make a trade, or send one of Big Daddy's bag men to do the dirty work.

Big Daddy had two sons working at the Port. One was fired twice while I was there for using drugs, fighting and stealing. The other son was running things when I left. I met his daughter while at work one day: she looked tougher than the boys. I am sure Jack "Big Daddy" Hornbeck had many scams; I was only involved with a few. The first I came across was the purchasing and equipment fraud. This one was pretty common and simple. The Port, like many city agencies, had its own purchasing department. This meant the individual department had their own vendors, their own oversight, and bills were paid within the department. The difference with the Port was that the maintenance department was not monitored by the City or the Port main offices up in the Ferry Building. The Ferry Building and Pier 46B were essentially two different departments. Big Daddy was in charge of purchasing, which also meant he was in charge of disposal.

Disposal went something like this: the Port needs a new backhoe. Jack says okay; the city buys the Port a backhoe. Now the old backhoe is old, but has very few hours on it because, well, there just was not a lot of work done. So the new backhoe comes. Taking the new one is too risky—even the most trustworthy Toady might blow the whistle on that—so you keep the new one, pretend to sell the old one to somebody, write down you sold the old one, or say nothing, but the backhoe goes with Big Daddy.

This kind of scam can be used for anything the city can buy, but Jack Hornbeck seemed to like equipment and tools, paper towels, water, toilet paper, and building materials. These were all loaded into the city's new pickup assigned to Jack Hornbeck. Jack's favorite bagman was Jerry. I kind of liked Jerry, and spent many hours counseling him on cronyism and stealing for other people. Alas, to no avail. Jerry was happy not to have to work to get ten hours of overtime now and then. All he had to do was fill Jack's truck a couple times a week, pick up checks, and deliver building materials to Jack's business partners at the wharf. In fact, almost all the workers at the Port were on the take, so to speak.

I learned a lot about corruption while working at the Port of San Francisco. One might think it would be difficult to have hundreds of people stealing and cheating the city out of hundreds of thousands of dollars each month, but it seems to work. The key is to piece off everyone. Like organized crime, you have got to give everybody a little taste. It is also very important to keep people scared, show the workers you could hurt them if they step out of line. The Cap helped with scaring people: he made them feel hopeless.

The Port didn't follow the city rules on discipline. Not long after I started I met a laborer who told me he was glad to be back to work. I asked where he had been. He told me he had been suspended without pay for twelve weeks. I said, "Good Lord, for what?" The laborer calmly stated he had gotten drunk at work and run a large "Port Packer," which is a giant forklift, into a wall and tipped it over. The laborer said he was just glad it had not gone on his record. I asked how it could have not gone on his record. The laborer told me the Cap suspended him with no hearing; nobody else was in the room; it was handled "in house."

Jerry the bagman was not a slow man. He seemed well dressed and well put together every morning. He never got dirty. I don't know if he was given a direct cut of the profits from Big Daddy, Inc. Jerry gave me a ride one day as I was walking down the Embarcadero promenade, coming back from lunch. I enjoyed the water and any chance I got I would walk along the San Francisco Bay under the Oakland Bay Bridge, all the way to Market Street some times. Jerry seemed puzzled when he picked me up, "What in the world are you doing walking around here; it's dangerous, you know." Yeah, I guess it could be, I thought. I had seen a lot of violence around here.

Years ago, I used to go over to Sausalito from the Ferry Building and "bird dog women." Before I would go I would always get pre-lubed at Fat Ron's, an old-time bar right under the freeway. It was just about the seediest bar in the city and a fight was always erupting. Outside loitered prostitutes, drug dealers, some homeless people, and sailors down on their luck, I did not use drugs or prostitutes but the area had a gritty flavor I enjoyed at times.

I got in the truck with Jerry the bagman and asked for a ride back to the shop. Jerry said sure. Jerry had a hard time with most of the workers because of his position with Big Daddy. Most of the other workers stayed clear, either out of jealousy or fear. It really did not matter. Jerry was hard up for conversation. Stacked next to Jerry's cleanly pressed Levis lay a stack of envelopes: all had Jack Hornbeck's name on them. There must have been ten or so. Jerry saw me looking and said they were Jack's checks. I said wow, that's a lot of checks. Jerry couldn't help himself, I guess. Big Daddy's bagman told me that, "The debris box company and Jack have a little side business going on. It must be a good one, 'cause I pick up a lot of these checks. The envelopes aren't always sealed." I flashed him a curious look, "Sometimes they are ten grand," Jerry said. "Damn! What in the world would that be for?" I asked. "It goes like this," Jerry said, his eyes lighting up, like he was talking about his war hero uncle. "Big Daddy orders twenty large debris boxes; the company bills for twenty large debris boxes; but only ten debris boxes come out to the port. The city pays the debris box company for twenty. Jack and the debris box company split the difference." "Shit!" I said. Jerry smiled proudly and dropped me off at Pier 46B, Port of San Francisco's maintenance department.

I never actually met Big Daddy, but he did speak to me once. I was assigned to build an office for the mechanics, sort of a clean room for their computer and record keeping. Barry, the newly divorced tenant of the break room, was assigned along with me. I never once saw Barry Manish anywhere near the job site. Big Daddy strode into the mechanics shop. Buddy was in charge there I was told, but Buddy had the alcoholism really bad and did not show up much. I was about half done with the project; my partner Barry was nowhere to be found. "Jesus Christ! You're not done with this yet? My daughter could build this faster!" Jack Hornbeck shot me an angry look and walked out. Big Daddy was big, well over six feet tall, and he carried himself like a Big Daddy. Having seen his daughter, I would agree. Jack Hornbeck retired a couple of months later, along with some more equipment and supplies. I never saw him again, although I heard his sons got in trouble again. The thieving druggy one got fired once more, I read, and the other one is no longer running things.

Chapter Ten

The Blade

This morning started like any

other morning. I rose about 4:45 a.m. in Petaluma, a nice little town about forty miles north of Pier 46B. I got dressed, kissed my three daughters and wife goodbye, and walked to the bus stop about a half-mile away. I arrived at Second Street, about one mile from work in San Francisco's South Beach area. I walked down Second Street, stopped at the Coffee Roasters, bought a cup of strong coffee and a scone. I headed down Second Street straight to the Bay and onto the Embarcadero. I usually arrived early. I like to have my coffee, eat a little something, and then have a smoke. This sends me to the men's room, where I catch up on some reading. I am always squared away and ready for work by 7:30 a.m.

This was never the case for my partner, Barry Manish. Apparently the ill effects of Barry's divorce were not yet gone. Every morning he made it in at all he was late and horribly hung-over, drunk, or high on a myriad of drugs, ranging from methamphetamine to weed. And he was a mean drunk too. The only time he was the least bit civil to me was when he was telling some story about either stabbing someone, kicking the shit out of someone, or doing some unspeakable degradation to some woman, since they were "all whores," as Barry the "Blade" Manish would exclaim if anyone had a nice thing to say about women in his presence. And he smelled. This guy was the filthiest working person I had ever met: his clothes were filthy; his hair was long, unkempt, and greasy; his complexion was bad, no doubt due to the drug use and drinking. The Blade would take out his Buck knife and pick at his sores. He would even run the blade along his cheeks to shave off the scabs. I don't know if people called him the Blade because of the body carving he did to himself with his Buck knife or because he bragged about the carving he did to others. Anyway, Barry Manish was a disgusting individual, and I had to ride with him every day he came to work.

One particularly bad day for the Blade, and an even worse day for some poor old lady coming out of the post office, we had just left the shop. The Blade had not gotten to work until noon, and boy was he drunk. Cam Stoutman ordered me to accompany Barry to some job out near Pier 80, almost back to Dog Patch, along the Third Street corridor. There was a large U.S. post office near by, and as the Blade rounded the corner, another driver was coming out of the parking lot. I saw the car ahead in plenty of time to slow down. I yelled for the Blade to stop. Bam!

We broadsided this lady and knocked her into next week. After a few minutes I got out to check on the lady in the car. She was hurt. I turned around to tell Barry to call an ambulance, but the Blade was gone. People from the post office who heard the crash came running out. I yelled for an ambulance and waited with the groaning victim. The ambulance and a Port truck came about the same time. The ambulance stopped at the scene but the Port truck kept going. The paramedics loaded the lady and drove off. Well, there I was, alone at the scene. The port truck's heavy bumper allowed very little damage to the city truck, but the lady's small compact was pretty bad. The cops showed up next. They asked me what happened: I felt they already knew. The police asked if I could drive. I said yes, and off I went in the Blade's brand new Port of San Francisco pick-up. I returned to Pier 46B. The Blade was gone. Cam Stoutman was not around. I waited several hours, then Kerry and Kimball returned about quitting time. Not a word was mentioned, and still no Stoutman. At 4:00 p.m. I punched out and went home. The Blade did not return to work for several days. When he did, Stoutman put me back working alongside Barry. I was cautious, knowing this guy could not be trusted.

One stormy Monday Cam Stoutman ordered Barry and me down to the Wharf to repair a seawall. After some planning and discussion, mostly between the backhoe operator and myself, Barry and I came up with a plan. One man would go down the ten-foot deep hole and build a form for a new concrete patch. The other man would watch the water level and for any other danger that might appear. "Get down in that hole boy," Barry yelled, so the equipment operator could hear him. Barry chuckled, as did the operator. "You're the new guy, get in that hole. I will hand you the tools and lumber." I reluctantly climbed the ladder down to water level. The Bay was slapping up against the rubble that doubled as the sea wall. Actually, the Bay spray as it filled the air brought me back to my days of sailing on the Bay, racing J 24's with my friends the Dalys, having drinks after the race at the yacht club.

The Blade didn't seem drunk this morning and had been pretty good the last couple of weeks, so I didn't mind. The way the break was situated under this pier at the wharf, I had to have my back to the Bay as I built my form. I yelled up to the Blade, "Make sure you keep an eye on this water and let me know if it starts coming in on me." The Blade said okay and I went to work. The smell of the newly cut lumber, the salt spray in the air, just being outside at Fisherman's Wharf, I felt a great deal of satisfaction being a carpenter. I was thirty years old but I had been a carpenter for fifteen years. There was not much I couldn't do when it came to building. This was the opposite of Barry Manish: there really was not much he could do. I wondered how he got a job there in the first place. The Blade had the new truck and new tools. Whenever Cam Stoutman would take off, Barry would be the boss. It just did not make sense: the Blade was a drunk, a druggie, he had zero people skills, and he smelled bad—a real embarrassment to the Port, I thought.

All of a sudden I was covered from head to toe with water. A big wave slammed me to the ground. I struggled to get up as another wave drove me to the ground. With the broken rubble smashing against my body, I yelled for help and looked to deck for the Blade. What the fuck? No Blade! I struggled to grab the ladder. Another wave knocked me over again, and again I was thrown against the rocks. As quick as it began it stopped. I righted myself with the help of the nearby ladder. I yelled for help, but still there was no help. As I reached the top, no one was around. No Blade. No operator. Not a soul. Some tourists, but damn few of them as the weather was bad and it was early morning, for tourists at least. I leaned against the Blade's new truck and found a semi-dry Newport in my shirt pocket. I took a long drag on my cigarette as I watched a huge ship pull away from the dock. I looked in the hole as the water filled the work area, dragging my skill-saw out to the Bay. Just in time, I thought.

About ten minutes later up walks Barry Manish and the worthless operator. They both looked puzzled at my disheveled appearance. As they got closer the Blade began to laugh, "Got wet, did ya?" "Fuck you, Blade, take me back to the shop, asshole." The Blade was a hard ass; he did not like to be talked to like that. "Fuck you!" the Blade answered. "Get the tools out of the hole and I'll take you back, ya pussy!" The Blade looked into the hole, "Where's the tools, asshole?" "Check up your ass," I answered.

Now the Blade did not like this, but the worthless operator did and laughed out loud. The few tourists who were down at the Wharf that day enjoyed our exchange as well. There were a few laughs from the crowd that had gathered. This angered the Blade a great deal; the Blade stomped over to me. The Blade Manish was about six inches taller than me, probably fifty pounds heavier, and he was not fat. I flicked my second cigarette away as he stormed over. I was about thirty years old, right around 5'9" if I stood straight, which had become increasingly hard these days for some reason.

My back hurt every day. I always attributed this to the fact I was a carpenter: carrying two hundred pound doors around, digging, and pounding nails everyday could probably explain this pain, I thought. I had a good build: wide shoulders, small waist, big legs, large forearms and shoulders, again from the work I did and genetics as well. I came from a long line of tradesmen. My great grandfather was a gifted carpenter, as well as my grandfather and uncle. The Blade stopped, looked me over, rather bored, and said, "The boy's got a mouth on him, don't he." I continued my relaxed stance. We stared each other down for an uncomfortable couple of minutes, until I asked, "Could you take me back to the shop, so I can get out of these wet clothes?" The Blade turned around silently and got in the new truck. I hopped in and off we went. Of course it was near enough for the Blade to get lunch, so we had to stop at El Faros on First Street to get his daily burrito.

By the time we got back the whole yard knew the story...or a story. I worked with Guadalupe Guadalupe, our shop man, for the rest of the day. I liked Guadalupe: he was from the Philippines. Having grown up in Daly

City, I was accustomed to Philippinos and I truly enjoyed their attitude toward life and its many challenges. The subject of the Blade came up more than once between Lupe and I. Guadalupe Guadalupe pretty much laughed out loud when I brought him up. I guess it would be funny if you didn't have to work with a violent, alcoholic drug user. And Lupe did not have to work with the Blade. Starting the next day, neither did I. The next morning Cam Stoutman informed me that I was to work with Kerry Greene.

Kerry Greene was a big guy. Everything was big with Kerry: his feet, his head, his hands, his shoulders, and his stomach. Kerry was very self-conscious about his weight. I am guessing his wife gave him a hard time, because no one else did, but Kerry always had a story about gaining weight. He went on a cruise and gained twenty pounds; he went out to dinner and gained twenty pounds; he drank beer all weekend and gained twenty pounds: if all these stories were true, he should be around five hundred pounds, not the heavy two hundred sixty or so he was. Kerry, and maybe his wife, were the only ones concerned about his weight. On a particularly hot day at Pier 46 we all had our shirts off at lunch, out behind the shop on the pier itself. Kerry was hunched over, trying to conceal his belly. Someone in the group mentioned his posture and asked why he was hunched over so. Kerry got extremely agitated and yelled fuck you to all who could hear. No one ever talked about Kerry's weight after that, except Kerry. The very first job Kerry and I were assigned to was a secret job—so secret, Cam Stoutman, the boss, would not even tell me. At the start of the day, usually around 8:30 a.m., after coffee and an extremely boring hour of tall tales, we all mounted our city trucks and went out to our assigned posts. Kerry and I were assigned to close out all the outstanding accounts we had at various lumber-yards around the Bay Area. Cam Stoutman did mention, as we were leaving, that if we did not use the accounts we would lose them. So off we went to South City Lumber.

We loaded up about $3,000.00 worth of clear redwood into the big ¾ ton truck. Then we drove straight over to a house in the Sunset district of San Francisco that be-longed to Kerry's mother, and Kerry unloaded his prize in the basement. I was afraid the neighbors would see us and call the Port, but Kerry did not seem to mind. Kerry Greene asked why I was not helping him unload: I told him I was not going to risk my job so he could steal. Kerry shook his head, finished his dirty work, and off we went to another store. We got some more of the people's goods and went back to Kerry's mom's house. This went on all day until the last load. It was nearing quitting time and I asked to be dropped off at the shop. Kerry complied. Kerry dropped me off in front of Pier 46B, then off he went again.

Poker Money

The next morning the truck was empty, but the chang-ing room at the carpenter shop was filled with workers smoking and playing cards. There was no ventilation in that little twelve by twelve room, and I could not get to my locker to suit up. I asked the workers what they were playing. A couple said "Crazy Eights." I asked if I could join them, and a few said sure. We played Crazy Eights for an hour or so; even the boss came in to play a couple of hands. This went on every morning, through lunch and break, and even from three in the afternoon until quitting time. This made it very hard to use the locker room for changing and taking breaks. I mentioned this to Kerry and Cam: they just shrugged. I thought this was something I had better get used to, but I had an idea. "Why don't we play Poker instead?" I asked. A silence fell over the group. Then people thought this might be a good change, so it began. Twenty-five cent limit, four raises, and it was dealer's choice. This became so popular that sometimes we would have two and three games going on in this little room. We put in a fan to clear out the cigarette and cigar smoke. I had another idea, which I brought up to Kerry and Cam Stoutman, the carpenter supervisor. "With all these people in our break room we should get something for our trouble. I mean, we have to clean up after these guys. We don't get to use our locker room and two to three hundred dollars goes through here every day." My father had taught my brothers and me how to play Poker from an early age. I had just won a Poker tournament at the "Spa," a local card room in Petaluma. I left that out of my presentation to Kerry and Cam. I got the okay from the big guys and a Poker room was born.

The games started at 7:00 a.m. Kerry or I was always on site. Fifty cents was pulled from each pot and put in a lockbox in Kerry's locker. At the end of the first day we had $50.00. Kerry took half that money and bought a couple cases of beer, which we then sold back to the Poker patrons for a dollar a piece, a nice profit. We took that money and put it back in the lockbox. Our Poker room was becoming very popular: the big bosses would play now and then and pretty much left it alone. Pretty soon we were knocking down $300.00 a day. The problem was, what in the world were we going to do with this money? I had another idea.

The carpenter shop had a party for everything: birthdays, divorces, Fridays, just about any excuse to go to lunch and drink alcohol. Every Friday we would go out to lunch, nice lunches too, in the financial district. We had high balls for starters, then steaks, fish, and good wine. The bill was always around $500.00. The problem was, while we were away, the Poker games were still going on and we had a trusted partner pulling money for the lockbox. We just couldn't spend the money fast enough. Sometimes we would have $3,000.00 in the lock box. The carpenter shop started to throw bigger parties. We would invite anyone who wanted to come to the lunches. Our tabs grew as well: sometimes $1,000.00 if we had a good crowd. The eateries were happy to see us, even if we did get out of line occasionally.

As I think back on this period, I recognize I made some mistakes. I was an excellent Poker player: I won most of the time, supplementing my carpenter pay with two to three hundred dollars a week. Most of the other players did not notice this, but the Blade Manish did.

Every chance Barry got he would take me on, and nine out of ten he would loose. Not big, just say $100.00 dollars a week. I got my other couple hundred from the other ten players. Then of course because of his drug and alcohol problems even Kerry would not let Barry near the lockbox. Barry seemed to focus his anger on me, though. I should have paid more attention to this looming problem, but I had my own issues; I was low man here. This card room was something I could bring to the table, so to speak. The Poker games and lunches gave me some balance, but they infuriated the Blade.

One of the reasons city jobs attracted such miscreants and thieves was that no matter what your standing was in the community or the class you were born into, once you started with the City and County of San Francisco you could attain seniority. Seniority meant everything: no matter what you did or did not do, it all came down to seniority. In the Blade's mind, I was eroding his away somehow, and he hated me for it. I got tired of Poker and the lunches and pretty much stepped out of that scene. The money was stolen and it ended. Barry Manish's feelings towards me only grew more toxic. Barry was missing more time than usual. Kerry bought a ski boat, then Barry did. Kerry built a summerhouse, so Barry did. I tried to stay away from Barry as much as I could, but it was hard. Barry would take the day off, get drunk, then bring his boat up to the back of the shop. He would hop off and walk around the shop areas boasting about his drinking and looking for a fight. I stayed as far away as I could from this madman. Since I was a father and husband and lived in Petaluma, the Blade focused on competing with Kerry Greene. I still felt it had something to do with me. I got the distinct feeling Barry Manish meant me harm.

River Café

In November of 1990 my wife and I leased a space in a new building in Petaluma. We borrowed $10,000 from the city credit union, got $10,000 from the owner of the building, and another $10,000 from our bank. In February of 1991, the River Café was born. We had a grand opening and the whole carpenter shop was invited. My partner Kerry Greene didn't come, but Cam Stoutman and Barry Manish made it. However, Barry's intentions were bad. He came in, looked around, shook his head and left. This began a new hatred of me and a competition. But I was wrong about Kerry and Cam Stoutman. The opening of this little coffee shop that my wife ran infuriated Kerry Greene and Cam Stoutman as well. I asked Cam if I could take some time off to help her get the place up and running, and he said okay. But the few hours during the first two weeks of the grand opening I did take off, Cam Stoutman docked my pay. He did not allow me to use my vacation or sick time. Cam cited the rules, telling me I did not fill out the proper paperwork. I was handed a paycheck with only half my pay. I found this odd, knowing that the Blade Manish rarely came to work and Kerry stole thousands of dollars in lumber. Guadalupe spent most of his time working on projects for the homes of our

co-workers, but I could not access my sick time and legal-
ly accrued vacation time for an honorable endeavor like
this. I found out a lot about Cam Stoutman that day—the
kind of coward he was. My paycheck was on the work-
bench with everybody else's on the morning of payday,
which was every other Friday. By the time I opened it
up; Stoutman was gone for a day of sitting at a coffee
shop with another well-known alcoholic, Deavors from
the sheet metal shop. A week earlier, Kerry Greene had
requested not to work with me because I did not "come to
work enough." I thought once I finished helping out my
wife that this would blow over; I was wrong there too.

I found Cam Stoutman and his wet brain stare near
Red's Java House and motioned to him that I would like
to talk. Cam stopped his truck and I walked over. I had
my check in my hand and Cam hopped out of his Ford
Ranger. Cam Stoutman was at least eight inches taller
than me and outweighed me by at least sixty pounds. He
was around forty. He was shaking like a leaf. I did not
know if he hadn't "got well" that morning or what, but he
was sweating profusely and stuttered out a whiney state-
ment regarding how the other carpenters didn't think
it was fair that I "got time off for the Café endeavor." I
shot back, "What business is it of theirs? This is between
you and me." Cam said, "This is just how it is." I tried
to reason with Cam Stoutman for a few more minutes. I
told him my family needs my paycheck. I told him I have
three children. Cam Stoutman wouldn't budge. I then
asked Cam why Barry Manish could come late, be drunk,
and sleep all day in the shop. Why could Kerry steal thou-

sands of dollars of lumber, but I could not take time off to help my wife? Cam stared at me coldly and said, "You know how it is Lloyd. As long as you show up you can do whatever you want." This didn't make much sense to me, but a lot of other things began to come clear. Barry hated me for a lot of reasons, most having to do with him. Kerry Greene may have detested me even more, but I did not know how much until a few months later.

Chapter Eleven

Assault at 46B

As I walked down Second Street,

the warm, sweet air filled my lungs. The aroma of fresh roasted coffee hung like a curtain separating downtown from the waterfront. The morning sky was awash in a scarlet sunrise. The morning of June 28, 1991 started no differently than any other workday for me. I got up at 5:00 a.m. to catch my bus to the city. I rode the 76 bus to Second and Mission. I got my coffee at the same roaster. I walked past the same blank stares of the heroin addicts at the methadone clinic. I passed the numerous city and county vehicles lining the street, city employees waiting for their dose. But when I entered Pier 46B a strange calmness surrounded me. Was I early, I wondered? Where was everybody? Then I looked over to the glass-walled offices that the crew bosses occupied. William O'Reily gave me a nod, but Gary Olson had his head in his hands and looked like he might have been sick.

As I walked into the massive shed where the craft shops were housed, the pungent odor of stale smoke and alcohol pierced my nostrils and upset my stomach. The usual sound of workmen talking before the morning whistle was absent this warm June morning. The giant shed seemed more like a deserted ballroom. As I turned the corner into the carpenters' shop, I noticed Lupe, the shop man, sitting alone at his table reading the morning paper. He too seemed awkwardly still. I opened the locker room door and nearly passed out from the smell. The stench in the air was so foul I gagged then cussed. I put my hanky to my nose and began to investigate. Beer cans, cigarette butts and half empty glasses of whiskey lay like dead soldiers amidst the stains and up-turned furniture. Wow, what a party I missed, I thought. In the six years I had been with the City and County of San Francisco I had seen many of these parties. Some were even funded by our gambling business. Retirements, birthdays, St. Patrick's Day, Christmas Eve, Thanksgiving, Thanksgiving eve, Friday eve, Friday, it did not take much to get a party going on city time. Sometimes, just two people thirsty would do it.

But this party was truly special; the Port had gone through one of the City's "reorganizations." These happen at a pretty regular clip. These reorganizations usually go like this: a consulting firm is hired; the City puts out a bunch of money; the consulting firm recommends some changes; the top brass get more money; some lower paid workers are laid off; and in a year things pretty much go back to where they were before. This one was a little different though, because things got shaken up a little more than usual. One foreman left his wife and kids for one of the consultants. Things could get a little messy, especially when someone tried to create change in a department like the Port. Side deals and money changing hands were the norm, and the big bosses like Stoutman and Gary Olson did not like change, especially if it meant they were going to have to put in a full day's work.

June 27, 1991 is when the word came down that more than a few supervisors were losing their jobs or being reassigned. The shit, or I should say the whiskey, really hit the fan. The word got around about 9:00 a.m. That morning by 10:00 a.m. the beer and whiskey were flowing at Pier 46B. My drinking alcohol at work days were behind me; I had a full day ahead of me. I had to finish work and then I had an appointment with an accountant to help with the paperwork and book keeping for the Café. Then I would mop the floors at the River Café, take out the garbage, and pick up supplies for the next day. So when the bottle of Jack Daniels was passed to me by Cam Stoutman at 10:00 a.m., I declined.

This was a mistake. I knew right away. A scowl came over Stoutman's worn out face, and Kerry Greene tossed me a beer. "At least have a beer ya cunt," Barry Manish slurred loudly. "Have it yourself," I said back to Barry as I tossed it over to the Blade. Barry let it fall and the Budweiser sprayed everybody within ten feet. Another mistake, I thought; you don't want to antagonize the Blade Manish ever, particularly if he has been drinking. The Blade started to talk about all the people he had beat up in his lifetime, the women he had defiled, and so on. It was time for me to go. I asked Cam Stoutman if he had any work for me. He said no, so I told Cam I had some windows I was working on from the day before and if it was all right, I would do that today. "I don't give a shit what you do," Stoutman replied, and off I went.

I returned to the carpenter shop at Pier 46B about an hour before quitting time. No one was there, not a soul. I changed out of my work clothes, washed up, and started my trek to the bus stop about two miles away. As I walked by the Boondocks Bar I looked up to survey the crowd. Lo and behold it was filled to overflowing with most of the personnel assigned to 46B. A couple of pile butts yelled some drunken greeting. The Blade gave me the finger, and a few other coworkers motioned me inside. I waved and continued my journey. I figured the fellas would understand—I mean, how long can you behave like this? I had things to do. I was trying to go somewhere in my life, trying to make something out of myself. I did not want to be an alcoholic like my father or his father. I was trying hard to live straight and good. I was wrong; in a criminal society, and the Port is a criminal society, if an individual refuses to participate in the criminal activities, he is distrusted and must be culled from the flock. A criminal's biggest fear is exposure; if not everyone is in on the game, there is a risk of exposure.

Mislov the ironworker was exposed. Mislov was from Poland, tall, and a raging alcoholic. Mislov would bring half gallons of cheap vodka into the ironworkers' shop and fill his "flaska," as he called the small metal container that got him through the day. Mislov would fill his container right on the bench in plain sight of anyone walking by. Of course he smelled really bad, just like he drank a quart of vodka a day, which he did. Then Mislov would pass out in the city truck at different locations throughout the waterfront. One time I saw him at the Levi's Plaza with his feet out of the window, snoring so loudly people on the street were looking in the massive city truck, at 11:00 a.m. Well, word got back to Gary Olson through a member of the public or a city official. Mislov the ironworker got a talking to. That's it—a talking to. Mislov came right to me. Mislov accused me of ratting him out. I could hardly contain myself; I was near comical breakdown. I said, Mislov, first, I would never rat anyone out; and second, everyone knows you drink, so you basically told on yourself. Mislov the Polish man's brain was so wet he did not quite get it and he left me alone, after he told everyone who would listen that I ratted him out. This did not affect my reputation much; I was already distrusted for not drinking at work and not stealing.

But that was not the biggest roadblock for Kerry and me. Kerry Greene loved money above all else—really sad, I thought. Kerry would get extremely upset if money was made around him by others; anyone else's good fortune was Kerry's bad fortune. The River Café was not on a paying basis yet and it wouldn't be for some time, but Kerry did not know that and I did not tell him. I really did not know how badly I was disliked until I returned to work the morning after the blowout party, June 28, 1991.

No one here, I thought, what a party this must have been. I still hadn't finished my windows, so out I went. I brought the antique windows back to the shop at 9:00 a.m. or so. I was restoring the century-old windows when Kerry Greene strolled in about 9:15 a.m. My relationship with Kerry Greene had been strained as of late, but I thought things were getting better. They were not.

Kerry gave me a nod and went into the break room. The next one to come in to work this sunny Thursday in June was the man himself, the Blade Manish, all six feet two of "lean mean nail driving machine," as he called himself, or B.A.M.: those were his initials. One morning I saw the Blade fabricating some metal in the carpenter shop. I asked what it was. Barry said it was a branding iron and he was going to "get it red hot and put it right on his girlfriend's butt." I about half believed him. Then again it was hard to figure out what was truth and what was fiction with the Blade. That same day he also explained in great detail why intravenously shooting methamphetamine and drinking alcohol was probably the best high ever. This was not a man to mess with, I thought. So as the Blade strode by me that fateful morning, lowered his trademark shades and shot me a bloodshot stare, a cold shiver went up my spine.

Cam Stoutman was nowhere in sight. Cam did not miss many days. No matter how hung over he was, he always made it in. Cam Stoutman must have been really sick this morning. Bad news for me. Cam Stoutman did not like me, but he was not dangerous or violent. The Blade hated my guts, was drunk, and in charge that day.

It was time card day. Oh boy, I thought, this could be trouble. As Barry rolled by, the dark brown circles under his eyes made his light blue eyes more fierce. "The fuck you looking at," Barry slurred as he swaggered by. I gulped and quickly returned to my task of rebuilding the antique windows at a nearby bench. Kerry and Guadalupe had already disappeared. Only Danny, the shop helper, was left to witness my murder, I thought. Then I heard it, "Get your ass in here and sign your time cards asshole," Barry yelled. Danny dropped his head and smiled. I tried to. I walked over to Cam Stoutman's office, a swank little twelve-foot by twelve-foot room looking out over the Bay, two big windows opening onto the pier deck. Normally I would be happy to sit in this nice little piece of heaven. But not today. I knew trouble was brewing.

Barry had been drunk for weeks and with the party last night I was sure he wasn't finished partying yet. The Blade would like to top this bender off with a good old fashion ass kicking with me as the guest of honor. I thought quickly on my walk to the office: just sign the card and get out of there. Don't say anything, don't argue, just take it and leave. If he tries to hit me, I'll duck and run. Who was I trying to kid? This was going to go bad. He could be armed with a knife, a gun, or a club. I thought about picking up a board for protection. Before I knew it, I was inside. For some reason, and I hope it was just nervousness or habit, I shut the door behind me.

There he was stretched out in Cam's big chair, feet on the desk, looking over aviator sunglasses, the whole office smelling like booze. I sat down in one of the three chairs pushed against the walls of the bright office. The Blade pushed my two timecards over to me without saying a word, just picking some sores on his arms and hands with a big knife. Before I could decipher the grade-school-like scribbles, the Blade stood up, leaned over the massive oak desk, and said, "I docked ya half a day yesterday for leaving early; I didn't see you after lunch." I don't really know what got into me, but I answered rather quickly, "How could you see me? You were at the Boondocks Bar all day." I knew it was a mistake when it came out. Barry Manish was around that big desk before I could get up out of the chair. "You are the biggest piece of shit in this whole pier." As I rose from my chair with the intent of backing out the door, I stared at the big knife Barry had laid down on the desk. Before I could straighten myself up the Blade delivered a blow that hit me square on the chin. I crashed into the wall with tremendous force. A large clock fell from the wall and hit my head, then my shoulder, nearly rendering me unconscious. As I looked forward, I saw Barry charging towards me. I put out my hands to cushion the strike. The Blade grabbed me by my jacket and threw me against the other wall like a rag doll. I crumpled towards the floor. For an instant I regained my composure and was able to shift his weight so we would not land on the floor. Unfortunately for me, a large wooden armchair was closest, and we ended up across that piece of furniture with me on the bottom. The Blade's face was nearly touching mine; his bloodshot eyes were wildly open, the stench from his breath was unbearable, there was a brownish liquid running from his nose, and the smell of old booze and body odor nearly made me vomit.

It was here that my spine was fractured. A searing hot pain was radiating across my back and chest: I could barely breathe.

I was able to squeeze out a pathetic "enough." The Blade got off me and walked casually over to the desk chair and sat down. Grabbing his knife, he resumed picking at some imaginary speed bug. Kicking the shit out of someone gave this miscreant no more discomfort than a mosquito bite. As I dragged myself towards the shop area, Danny Jamali shot me a panic-stricken stare. I gingerly made my way to the break room. As entered the small room I nearly fell to the dirty floor. Kerry Greene was resting and reading the paper. He barely looked up as I vomited in the sink over and over. I turned to Kerry and asked if he would drive me to the hospital. He said no and left the room. I steadied myself against the sink and heard a knock on the door. I couldn't make it over to the door. It slowly opened. Danny stuck his head in, " You okay buddy?" I asked if he would drive me to the hospital. "Yeah, sure, I'll get the truck," Danny yelled. Danny helped me to the truck and we left for the workers' clinic at a nearby hospital.

Chapter Twelve

Back to School

"You shouldn't turn down too
many more of these jobs, Mr. Kraal," the nice tall judge
said to me. This was 1994 and I had just spent three and
a half years trying to regain my health after the assault
at the Port. My broken back had mended, but it was stiff
and painful. I was fearful of the city but couldn't get another job because of my back. I had tried to go back to
the Port, but I was nearly killed on several occasions.
I had won in court and the jury voted unanimously in
my favor, awarding me all my back pay and my doctors'
bills. The city paid the judgment, but there were a lot of
bruised egos at the Port. I was nearly run over by Cam
Stoutman, my former foreman at the Port, one morning.
I had to dive over some landscaping and onto the pave-
ment to avoid the blue city truck roaring towards me at
sixty miles per hour. I filed a police report, but the Port's
human resources department threatened to fire me if I

didn't recant my testimony. I refused, and they laid me off. When the city put out the carpenters' hiring list, I was number one, so the first opening to come up in late 1994 was mine if I wanted it.

A short time later a letter came from the City and County offering me a carpenter job at the San Francisco Unified School District. I remembered the nice judge at the Workers' Compensation Board and his advice to me. After all, he came out on my side in a hearing against the city. The city attorneys sent three lawyers up to Santa Rosa to argue that I shouldn't get workers' compensation for the injuries I received when my Port boss beat me up. I was by myself, three against one. I stated my case. I told the judge I had a verdict from twelve jurors. I told him these twelve jurors placed the blame for my injuries on the drug and alcohol induced attack by my supervisor at the Port of San Francisco. The judge quickly found in my favor and boy, were these three attorneys upset.

Attorneys don't like losing, especially not to a carpenter with a twelfth grade education. They really hated that ruling and me, as it turned out. The judge awarded me $10,000.00, and of course told me to take the next job the city offered me. I did this and went down to the School District. I was thirty-five now, and this back disease was taking its toll on me. My neck was sore and stiff all the time. My back had twisted and grown bone over the fracture I received from my Port of San Francisco supervisor. I did not sleep well and I still had some anxiety about the experience I had at the Port of San Francisco. But we needed the money. Although the River Café was able to feed my family, my children were becoming teens and we needed more income. So, I felt I would try again. When I entered this old shop I was directed to a very short Latin man. I introduced myself and got a long, bored look from this stranger. I don't think the foreman was quite five feet tall, but he had on these cowboy boots with silver tips and decorative spurs. His hair was perfect and he spoke very bad English. When he shouted, he would ready himself from about ten feet away, scream some directions at me in broken English, and then quickly go to his office, shut the door and lock it. Usually I was alone with him when he did this. I never quite got it until another carpenter happened to witness this bizarre behavior. I asked my new co-worker what he thought it was all about. Well, my co-worker said, "We heard you killed your last boss and I think he is afraid of you." I laughed out loud and so did the carpenter. I told him the story from the Port and we all had a good laugh.

Manny Pena, the spur-wearing foreman, did not laugh. Manny was upset with me. Manny had a slow nephew trying to get a permanent city job and felt I was taking his job, I was told. I tried to be respectful to Manny but he made it really hard. Every crummy job Manny would give me and every chance Manny got he would criticize my work. I wasn't allowed to drive a vehicle and many times I would have to take the bus to my assigned post because he would hold me up at the shop until the other workers had left. After the other crews had gotten their assignments and were off, Manny would suddenly tell me, "Oh I forets Mifter Royd, yuse go to Leecon wiff Randy." I would inquire how I was supposed to get there and he would smile and state, "I dun care," and retire to his office, of course locking the door. And then Manny would discipline me for not being on site on time.

Most of the carpenters hated Manny Pena, but they still worked on his personal house because if you did not, you got the worst duty. I refused to work on his personal residence. So a few of the workers like me worked on our hands and knees in the bathrooms of the high schools. Another time, Manny gave the wrong instructions to a co-worker, which the co-worker passed on to me. When I completed the task I was written up and recommended for termination. This co-worker I enjoyed a great deal. He was nearly seventy years old. This man was the temporary foreman for many years, and thus he presented a danger to Pena. So Manny, the gentleman that he was, would have this seventy-year-old man work on his hands and knees in every disgusting, dirty toilet the San Francisco School district had. A few days later, I was suspended for receiving workers' compensation while working, another clerical mistake, I was told. But the suspension stayed and I lost a week's worth of work and pay. I wasn't allowed back until they straightened it out. One of the ladies in accounting at the School District slipped and told me she gotten the information from the Port and the City Attorney's office. They were still upset with me because they lost twice in court. I protested and pleaded with the School District for my lost week's wages. To no avail— they presented me with termination papers.

The City Attorney assigned to carry out the firing was a girl I went to grammar school with. I told her that Pena was a liar; I told her he had been setting me up since I got there. I told her that he required the workers to work on his house and if they didn't they got bad duty. Manny Pena was a despicable human being; he abused his power and took advantage of the most vulnerable workers. If you did not help him steal he would try to fire you. My argument was rejected and the School District fired me. I appealed the ruling to the San Francisco Civil Service Commission and they reversed the School District's decision. They offered to put me back on the carpenters' hiring list if I agreed not to seek work with the School District. I agreed and filed a federal lawsuit for discrimination. I told the federal judge that the Port and the City Attorney's Office, along with the School District, conspired to fire me from the School District and separate me from city employment because of my injuries at the Port.

I prevailed again, and another group of city attorneys hated my guts. I wasn't wrong about Manny Pena though. Manny Silver Spur was fired from the city a few years later for stealing and lying. But he got his job back, because he threatened to blow the whistle on his bosses.

Chapter Thirteen

Cable Cars

Two years had passed since I
had left the School District, and I was frantically trying
to find work other than with the City and County of San
Francisco. I was working at the River Café and things
were going all right. I had just finished my first two years
of college and I was accepted into the C.B.A. law school in
Santa Rosa. I was coaching my daughters' sports teams
and I was content. About the same time I found out how
much law school was going to cost, I got another letter
from the City and County of San Francisco. I was being
offered a job at the Cable Car Barn on Mason Street in
San Francisco. I remembered the round brick building
where I found Merricik the carpenter passed out in the
back of his truck some fifteen years ago. I enjoyed the cable cars. What a prestigious job for a carpenter, I thought.
After all, these historic old cars were like pieces of art
rolling up and down my beloved city. I suddenly got ex-

cited! Maybe they had forgotten about me and the Port? Maybe I could just be one of the guys.

It is funny how our minds work: just a few short years away from the madness I had fond memories of my work with the city. I talked it over with my wife. We looked at our finances and said yeah, maybe I would give it another try. I was worried about my back and neck though. This disease they found when the druggie beat me up was getting worse. I was in almost constant pain and I was very stiff. I researched the Americans with Disabilities Act and thought I could go in, interview for the job, tell them about my back and neck, and see what they said. But the way the rules work, you must accept or turn down the job first. I took it and went in for my interview.

I told the huge lady that I had Ankylosing Spondylitis and I could do the work, I would just need some reasonable accommodations. She said okay right away and sent me to the doctors for a physical. The doctors at General Hospital held me up for a month or so. I later found out the supervisors at the barn did not want me there and they were lobbying hard to keep me out. Lucky for me though, the same supervisors were known racists, and the lady who was helping me was black and did not much care for our white supremacist adversaries. So, after a couple of months of negotiating, I was hired under the Americans with Disabilities Act as a carpenter at the cable car barn working for the Municipal Railway of San Francisco.

It was a nightmare from the very beginning. But some good things came out of it: I bought another piece of property and went to Europe for the first time. I took my three daughters and my wife for nearly a month. I worked some overtime, when I wasn't going to law school. Many of the workers, seeing me doing my legal studies homework at lunch, started asking me for legal advice on divorces and home loans. I helped one guy get out of a messy lawsuit; another guy had me review his divorce settlement. We made some changes and both parties were very happy—so happy, they wanted to give me money. I turned it down, thinking I would rather have allies. I told them you wouldn't want a brain surgeon only halfway through with medical school, would you?

Unfortunately, things started to come unglued shortly after that. The people who had approved my hiring either retired or quit. My back was getting worse and my old friend Merricik, the alcoholic drug addict, was feeling threatened because I placed higher than him on the carpenter supervisor's test. I placed number seven out of a hundred and fifty, and Merricik was near the bottom. Tests came easily to me: I had been in college now for nearly five years and had a year of law school under my belt. On the other hand, Chip Merricik, my supervisor, could neither read nor write. Merricik had been working on the bosses' houses and properties pretty steadily for fifteen years, if he wasn't too drunk, and damn it, if there was a supervisor's job to get, he would get it. I thought I had learned my lesson by now. The city and I were not a good fit. This was 2000 and I had started in 1985. I thought if I could just get through college and law school I would leave for good, but being a carpenter was all I knew. With my deteriorating body I would have to use my brain. I thought I needed to get some training to move on.

We got two new bosses to take the place of the one who retired, the nice old guy I knew from my stint at the cable car shop in Dog Patch. Dan Lobo's replacements were really a couple of beauties. One, Joe Randall, came to work usually at about 9:00 a.m. Joe smelled so much like booze it would knock you over. The other guy, Jimmy Chang, seemed like he might have been mentally retarded. Within the first week of being on the job, Jimmy Chang had wrecked the entire fleet of city vehicles assigned to the shop, including the tow trucks, and hurt himself. Joe Randall was found to have brought a loaded handgun to work one day. He smelled so much like booze that the security personnel came down to the shop, threw him against the car, frisked him, removed the gun, and then we did not see him for some time. These were the bosses.

The workers, especially Chip Merricik, were even more bizarre. Chip Merricik, because of his willingness to work on the supervisors' houses and properties, of course was our foreman. He made the most money and could smoke weed all day long without worry of exposure or discipline. This was bad for Merricik, mostly because he was not very bright to begin with and when he was high he talked and appeared to be someone with a brain injury, which may have been the truth. Chip also shot heroin and had contracted Hepatitis C. Most of the bars in Merricik's hometown were filled with cable car parts and priceless memorabilia Merricik had traded for free drinks, drugs and as payment for his many gambling debts. I remember one instance when Merricik had us remove the entire front of a cable car and replace it with a new front. I assumed there was rot, but this one was perfect. I put a hold on the job. I told Merricik that we must have the wrong car: this one was fine. Merricik just chuckled with red eyes and said, "Get back to work," and went back to sleep in the rear of the shop. The next day the new guy, a temporary carpenter, was loading that brand new cable car front in the back of Merricik's truck bound for some gin joint in Sonoma or Lake County. It took three carpenters and a painter six months to rebuild the front of that cable car. I don't know how long I could have stayed there under these circumstances, but the City Attorney's office found out I was at the cable car barn and promptly came down and removed my A.D.A. status. I was then put in charge of replacing the bumpers on the entire fleet of the historic San Francisco Cable cars.

Take a look at the bumpers on these four thousand pound behemoths the next time you are in the City by the Bay. Undressed they weigh in the neighborhood of four hundred pounds. After the iron and add-ons they are close to six hundred pounds. At first glance one might think, wow, what a prestigious job, except I was told by a smirking Jimmy Chang I was to do the bumpers by myself and, "Do not under any circumstances bother the rest of the crew, as they have their own jobs to do." This was quite a project, and above all else, I am no quitter.

The last big project I got at the cable car barn had

been a year or so earlier. The previous boss had asked me if I could figure a way to organize accident and injury paperwork on the fleet of cable cars. "Presently every piece of information on the maintenance and repair of our cable car fleet is hard copy strewn around the greasy shop in assorted boxes," Dan Lobo stated. Whenever the claims department came down to the barn to get information on a car in an accident or an injury, which was often, it was a huge production that took days and days to locate the appropriate documentation. A great deal of fabrication was required as well, since no one kept good records.

I created a computer filing system that included all forty some odd cable cars; all of their maintenance records; all their accident reports, complete with pictures and witness testimony; names of the operators and conductors; their statements and their accident records. This program made it possible to search by a vehicle or an individual, including the maintenance mechanic or carpenter who had worked on the individual car. My boss was very happy with this work, but he retired soon after I completed it. The new bosses promptly told me they would not need me to update the files, as they had already "had this idea," and they would take over. They passed my work off as their own. I did not really mind; sitting in the office with the retarded guy and the human booze rag was too horrible of a thought.

In the meantime, I was installing four-hundred-pound bumpers by myself on the cable cars. The workers I had helped with their legal problems would slyly give me assistance every chance they got, at some expense to themselves. Everyone knew I was being punished; for what, no one really knew or cared. But they helped me anyway. Jimmy Chang would yell and scream in his heavy Chinese accent, stutter, and demand these workers do their own work. They would slowly comply as they touched my shoulder. It was obvious this work was taking its toll on me: I looked like I had a bad back and neck. I limped and my neck was frozen stiff. But I was not a quitter and as long as I could work I was going to work, and I was getting them done.

After a few of them, I figured out a system that involved tables and pattern apparatuses to aid my broken back and stiff neck. Jimmy Chang and Joe Randall did not like this. They were hoping this job would run me off, get me hurt, maybe kill me—they did not care as long as I was out of there. "No cripple is going to work here," they would say. Joe Randall always thought I was to blame for his firearm arrest and he was right. When I heard from one of his golf buddies that he would like to see me dead, I thought back on the gun I had found in his truck. The shells in his desk and, of course, him being drunk all the time, got me a little nervous. So yeah, I called security. I checked in with them a couple of days after they hauled him away. The nice lady said he admitted having the loaded gun. Joe Randall said it was a mistake to keep it in his desk at work or the city truck and he promised not to do it again.

I was given more work in between bumpers and my back and neck were failing fast. One particular day, close to quitting time, as I changed into my street clothes

Jimmy Chang came over to my locker and angrily asked, "What are you doing? We have got to get this car out." I calmly told the drooling foreman all right, and hurried to cut the heavy floor. My hand slipped and I was cut deeply on my left hand. I was always careful at work and this injury was my first in many years. I quickly wrapped a rag around to stop the bleeding, but soon the rag was soaked in blood. I was losing a lot of blood and I made a big mess on my way to Jimmy Chang's office. "Now what Lloyd?" Jimmy said in a bored manner. I told Jimmy I needed to go to the hospital. "Not until you fill out these forms, Lloyd." I was growing faint from the loss of blood. I was able to sign my name to the injury report, but covered it with blood.

I was taken to the hospital and after several surgeries and a couple of months of a soft cast; I was back at the cable car barn. And right back to the speed up and four-hundred-pound car bumpers. I was paid less than the other carpenters and I was a little cranky one day. Merricik thought it might be fun to forget some of my hours and my check was several hundred dollars short. I protested vigorously and my heroin-shooting boss offered to hit me in the face if I did not shut up about the pay shortage. I left and took this up with Jimmy Chang and Joe Randall, who was lying across his desk in the office. I was disciplined for this outburst and suspended for several days without pay.

I was having a lot of trouble with my back disease. One of the symptoms was eye infections. Because of these eye infections it became difficult for me to see. The cable car barn was kept dark for the sleeping night crew mechanics, if they were there at all. Many times the night crew would come to work, punch in, and then go home and sleep. This practice was stopped for a time when one of the mechanics, having over slept, came to the barn in a hurry and forgot he was in his pajamas. One morning when I punched in at 6:00 a.m., I had difficulty seeing in the dark. I punched my timecard on the wrong line and I was recommended to be suspended. William Tremmings, the racist who worked so hard against my hiring at the cable car barn, had taken an interest in my separation from city employment. William Tremmings and Joe Randall, the drunken, armed boss, elicited a city attorney by the name of Russell Lee. I was summoned to a meeting in William Tremmings's swank office on the mezzanine level of the barn. Bob Johnson was there as well; the Polaroids of his prepubescent Thai conquests were tucked safely away in the breast pocket of his oversized leather jacket.

I explained the eye infections common to this chronic disease; I presented my longtime Kaiser doctor's recommendation, that better lighting could aid my aim on the timecards. But Muni's diligent senior staff would have none of it. I was told my duties would be expanded. I was to report to the cable car shop on Minnesota Street in the mornings and clean up after the previous workers. I was then instructed to report back to the cable car barn to sweep up after the carpenters there. I did this and endured a great deal of ribbing from my coworkers. Both shops were cleaner than they had been for decades, I was told by the workers.

During this time another city worker thought he might take a crack at me as well. The most common trait I found, in the eighteen or so years of employment with the City and County San Francisco, was the victimization of the weak or the perceived weak. Pablo Gueterez was the shop steward for the cable car mechanics, thus he was allowed certain privileges and special treatment. Usually Pablo would exercise his immunity in the realm of drinking alcohol while on duty or remaining AWOL from work for weeks at a time during the many stints he spent in jail for immoral behavior. Without any threat of discipline from the bosses, Pablo Gueterez was a dangerous foe. Although we got along for the most part, Pablo was quick to pounce on the downtrodden.

I was an easy target: limping, having trouble seeing around the cable car shops, and busy cleaning up after the other workers I had bested on so many of the city's supervisor tests. And pounce he did. Pablo was allowed to schedule overtime and fill out the payroll paperwork, not only for the mechanics but the carpenters as well. Pablo was also a drinking and drug using buddy with my illiterate heroin addict boss, Chip Merricik. And of course Merricik was upset with me for several reasons, the biggest reason probably being that I finished higher than him on the supervisor's test. Pablo Gueterez thought it would be entertaining to forget most of my pay. I protested, but to no avail; trying to get your payroll mistakes fixed at Muni could take months, and that's if you did not lose your desire after ten weekly calls to payroll. It started to become clear to me that I wasn't going to be able work at the San Francisco cable car barn. Then I got an interview for a supervisor's job with the San Francisco Municipal Railway.

I had only slim competition: a carpenter who had started with Muni a few years earlier who couldn't really do carpenter work. Roger interviewed right before me. As he walked by me at the end of his turn in the pickle barrel, the poor guy was covered in sweat: his shirt was soaked and he shook as he walked. When we talked the next day he thought his chances were bad as he had no supervisor experience, and really was not a carpenter. Roger confessed he had worked with his father installing bathroom tiles and only got the carpenter job through a relative. But the fix was in, I thought, and I was right; the carpenter supervisor's job went to my sweaty tile setter co-worker. I was disappointed and my back and neck had worsened with the renewed heavy lifting and cleaning. It was time for another big decision.

The thought of cleaning up after my high and drunken coworkers for another twenty years was a prospect I found hard to face. I had accrued some vacation time, so I took my family to the island of Malta. I rented a farmhouse in a remote village on the island of Gozo. I felt I found some clarity in this far-off place spending hours watching the fishing fleet on the blue Mediterranean with my farmer neighbors. I spent another week in Paris and returned home refreshed and renewed. I realized the City and County of San Francisco was not going to give me a chance at the supervisor's job I had earned. And it was too late to start working on the bosses' houses. I resigned my position with the City and County of San Francisco. The very next day I started as a construction project manager for a local construction company.

Chapter Fourteen

Back
at
the Zoo

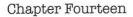

After working in private industry
for a few years, I started looking for something more ful-
filling. I was making a lot of money, but the work was
high pressure and not very rewarding. I started going on
the San Francisco Zoo website to check for openings. I
applied for everything they had. Finally, a Maintenance
Supervisor position came up. I was perfect for the job,
and was looking forward to being able to fulfill my life-
long dream of working at the zoo. I was excited and optimistic. I thought the zoo would be differet. Sure, it was a
large public organization, much like the City and County
of San Francisco, but it was managed by a non-profit—
the San Francisco Zoological Society. I was confident I
could excel at the zoo. I could fix the construction and
maintenance departments. I had worked very hard to
educate myself in construction management. I carried a
California State contractor's license, and I had managed

millions of dollars in construction work. I had recently estimated fifteen million in public works projects just like the work that was going on at the zoo. I knew it was a good fit and I would be able to make a positive impact. I have never been as wrong about anything as I was about the San Francisco Zoo.

The Walk Around

On my first day, my supervisor Candy Shultz instructed me to tour the grounds with her. She introduced me around then invited me to lunch with her in a private room off the back of the Leaping Lemur Café. It was uncomfortable, mostly because there were plenty of seats outside in the common area, but she insisted on buying lunch and sat very close to me, smiling, and talking low in a sort of baby talk.

But really, it was the "walk around" that was the most disturbing. We first talked about the crew I would be supervising and how they were ignorant, liars, badly trained, drug users, and lazy, with the exception of one individual, who had been granted five weeks off prior to my arrival. Candy Shultz described the maintenance crew as a most unproductive group, mostly illiterate, prone to mistakes and drug use. There was a married couple assigned to the maintenance crew, and I thought it was odd to have a married couple in the same department.

We then went by the grey seal enclosure: a sad, dilapidated space with a dry pool and overgrown shrubbery around the exterior. Candy informed me that this seal was old and blind, and probably would not live much longer. Candy Shultz stated: "It would not be wise to expend any money or energy on this animal." We then went to the Baird's tapir area; his pool drain needed repair and would not open. A tapir only craps in water, in order to throw off his predators in the wild. So the keeper had to drain and fill this 20,000-gallon pool whenever it needed to be cleaned. Candy assured me that the animal keepers were lazy and complainers; furthermore, we had only one Baird's tapir, a male. Candy informed me that because we had only one, and not a breeding pair, this creature was worth very little and the director himself, Carlos Casseris, didn't want anything done to this enclosure that would expend any money. And that is why we would not work on the valve.

Next we entered the Lion House. Candy pointed out that a local company had been working on the shift door mechanisms. The work was done with much displeasure from Candy, as she informed me that the Lion House keepers, not unlike all the other animal keepers at the zoo, were lazy, and they kept filing workers' compensation claims. "You seem distracted. Am I not interesting enough for you, Lloyd," cooed my new boss. "Oh, no," I said, "I was just thinking about all the work to be done here." Really I was thinking, did I make a mistake?

The Zebra Barn

Candy walked me back to our trailer and promptly told me I did not have an office right now, and would probably work out of the maintenance barn. I thought it was time to meet the crew I was assigned to manage. I made my way to the maintenance building, which happened to be the former Zebra Barn. The shop was adequate enough: somewhat small, but it could work for now, I thought. When I arrived I radioed the crew to meet at the shop. Peter, Renee and Jimmy showed up a few minutes later. Peter was a man in his late forties, I estimated. He chain-smoked and he had a nervous look about him. Renee, a female around thirty, I thought, and her husband Jimmy both looked like they might have been in a punk rock band. Their clothes were torn and stained. Renee had long, unkempt black hair. Jimmy had a neck tattoo, a shaved head and a long, strange goatee that only covered the end of his chin.

I introduced myself and told the crew I was very happy to be there. I told them drugs and alcohol would not be tolerated, nor would violence of any kind. No guns or knives were allowed at work and people would be expected to show up on time and work their entire shift. When I finished, Jimmy became agitated. Jimmy stepped close to me and raised his voice regarding some inequity done to him in the past. I didn't quite understand what he was talking about and his wife and Peter asked him to quiet down. Then, Renee started in on the bad treatment she had been getting. I assured the crew that people would be treated fairly, and as long as everyone did their job, things would be fine. We had four other people on the crew, I was told: Mo, Bob, Jacques and Boris. They were absent that day.

Before I went home from my first day of work at the San Francisco Zoo, July 3, 2006, I went to the assigned work areas of the three maintenance workers who showed up that day. I couldn't find Renee or Jimmy, but Peter was easy to find and eager to share his opinions on the other personnel and management. Peter told me Renee knew nothing about maintenance and Jimmy had anger issues that he had been written up for previously. Peter also was eager to share his drug use. Along with the others, he smoked marijuana daily. The rest of the crew was on meth and weed. I acknowledged this information but showed no outward concern. But inwardly I was thinking, Good Lord, here we go again. Is every city institution filled with violent, drug using, ill qualified miscreants, posing as employees? I tried to convince myself that these were probably the ramblings of that other city type: the sycophant or ass kisser, if you will. Still, I thought it would be wise to check around and see if there was any validity to these statements.

I first went to my new baby-talking boss, Candy Shultz, and asked her about the drug use and Peter's credibility. I got a mixed message from Shultz. First she said Peter was a liar, could not be trusted, and he was at the top of her "Hit List" as well as the Zoological Society's because he had won an award from an E.E.O.C.

claim he had made against the zoo and Candy Shultz. She then went on about the blatant and serious drug use within the maintenance department. Candy spoke about Jacques, the maintenance worker who was on an extended vacation she had granted him. Jacques was her lead person when she was in charge, and by Candy's account he was the only one on the crew who should not be fired. Well now, we are getting somewhere, I thought. So I said, "You know the crew does drugs." "Oh yeah," Shultz answered, "Many times Jacques would come up and report they were either smoking weed or using meth in the shop, sometimes openly dealing with other workers, making sales." "Wow," I said, "What did you do?" She said, "By the time I got down to the shop area, nothing was going on." Here we go again, I thought. Typical city job.

Grizzly Gulch

Shortly after I started in July of 2006, I was instructed to estimate the construction cost of the new Grizzly Gulch project. I was excited and anxious to showcase my talents as an estimator and project manager. I spent many long hours compiling bids and performing cost analyses for this new exhibit, "Grizzly Gulch." It was this honorable intention and task that certainly spelled my doom at The San Francisco Zoo. Grizzly Gulch had been in the works for some time, a few years at least. A drawing was accepted and a contractor was bidding on this project. After an outside firm was selected to estimate the project according to the drawings and specifications, the selected construction contractor gave the zoo a budget of almost three times the 1.8 million the consultant estimated. This is when Willy Ramirez, the Operations Director, asked me to estimate and obtain some other bids for this relatively simple project. So, I decided just what type of work this project entailed, and then set about selecting a contractor.

I selected a very well known firm in the Bay Area that I had worked with previously. The earlier project was very similar in scope. We had gotten that difficult job done for about a million. We thought we could probably complete this one for about one and a half. I was very excited about this news. I gave the good news to my supervisor Candy Shultz first. Little did I know that Willy's asking me to look at this project again had infuriated my supervisor Candy. She didn't show it right off though. I always kind of envied a person who could hold in their feelings and work behind the scenes towards an adversary's demise.

I soon found out that the San Francisco Zoo senior management is a fractured, incompetent group. Not unlike the City and County of San Francisco management I knew so well: a redundant team of ill qualified imposters mired in bureaucratic nonsense. A huge discrepancy existed at the zoo between the well-qualified and educated animal keepers and the senior staff. The keepers performed serious and dangerous tasks competently every day, day in and day out. I had never, in thirty plus years of working, been associated with so many dedicated and knowledgeable, but underpaid, people. Conversely, the senior staff buzzed in and out of the zoo in their expensive German cars, and collected huge salaries as new buildings paid for by hard-fought bond measures deteriorated daily, due to mismanagement and neglect.

At the San Francisco Zoo there are thousands of systems, ranging from state-of-the-art heating and ventilation to archaic machinery and tools. There are door closers, fire alarms, water heating, filtration systems, shift doors to insure safety for the public as well as the animals and keepers, and of course cages and moats, concrete bunkers and huge pools, miles of utilities for water delivery and sewer lines, natural gas lines and massive electrical panels and transformers. Each and every one of these systems requires a great deal of expertise to maintain and repair. At the San Francisco Zoo, with the exception of myself, there was no one even remotely qualified to perform this work. All the while, these new buildings and old exhibits were weakening—some beyond repair— and some never finished from the huge rebuilding over the last twenty or so years. The senior staff, led by an executive director earning a hundred thousand more a year than the mayor, appeared to be bent on increasing membership and attendance above all else. Marketing and development budgets ballooned as the animal care and building and grounds maintenance worsened.

Soon after my appointment, in cooperation with the animal staff, I presented a plan to maintain the zoo. I thought my two supervisors, Candy Shultz and Willy Ramirez, might storm out of the room. I was surprised they objected so vehemently and asked both if the animal keeper assigned to a particular animal was not the individual who would know the most and be the best informed regarding the animal's maintenance needs. Stunned silence followed, until finally Candy said, "The veterinarian is the expert." The good doctor was referred to by most of the staff as "Doctor Death." It should have been "Doctor Do Nothing."

I remember a very enlightening interaction I once had with the good doctor and his fellow city worker assistant, an extremely unpleasant woman who gained some notoriety by raising a polar bear at home. I was in the middle of a ten day straight stint, working very hard to fix the plethora of deferred projects, primarily a forty-foot abandoned trailer parked in the zoo commissary area that had become the home of thousands of rats that invaded and fouled the food supply for the animals. This trailer had been out of use for ten years before I was allowed to hire the appropriate company and perform the necessary preparations to have it removed. The aging and rat-infested animal hospital was located not ten feet from the rat hotel.

I had been summoned by the unpleasant woman to investigate some heating issues. I politely gave my best estimate on when and how we could rectify the heating problem. The two long-time city workers suddenly erupted in unison: "The maintenance here at the zoo is a disgrace," the ragged woman screamed, coming closer to my face. "You know we have rats scurrying above my head as we do surgery on these animals." The doctor yelled, "Your crew is high most of the time, and haven't done anything for this hospital since I've been here." The woman yelled, "This place is a disgrace!" The duo spoke in unison. I calmly asked, "How long have you been here?" The woman said, " Near twenty years." The doctor fell silent. I told the two that I had been here only a few months and I was trying very hard to fix things. I then asked them if things have been so bad for so long, why had they not complained, threatened to quit, make a report—anything. The unpleasant lady stormed off, having vented her anger of twenty years. The doctor excused himself as well. I found this older gentleman to be a likeable fellow, one more tired city worker trying to play out his career with as little commotion as possible.

Chapter Fifteen

Meth Heads at the Zoo

Biker Bob

"Hey Bob, looks like we got a new sheriff," the chatty, chain-smoking conman yelled as a very tall man with a long black ponytail strolled towards the shop area and former Zebra Barn. It was 8:30 a.m. and the morning meeting was coming to a close. This was our first official morning meeting since I had been hired as maintenance supervisor at the San Francisco Zoo. I had set it for a day when everyone was working, or so I thought, and I made it for 8:15 a.m. to give everybody time to get in and prepare. I held it at the shop in order to get acquainted with the crew in a more casual setting than the weekly meetings my predecessor used to have in a large trailer in the administration area, complete with pastries and coffee. This seemed like a great idea, but it hadn't been working. The first day I arrived, my direct supervisor, Candy Shultz, confessed to me she would like to see all the maintenance workers fired, with the exception of Jacques. I had yet to meet Jacques because Candy had given him six weeks off. This worried me some, because she kept professing her deep respect and affection for Jacques, saying he was the only worker with maturity and skill, and how happy I would be with him. I thought, if this guy is so important to the running of this shop, why did you grant him six weeks off the day I started?

My reflections stopped abruptly as I sensed the big biker staring down on me with a fresh cup of coffee. Bob was about six feet tall and he wore big boots with high heels. I was standing downhill from him, so he towered over me. I greeted Bob and explained plainly that he had missed most of the meeting, and I expected him to start on time: 8:00 a.m. The talkative, twitchy, short, cigarette smoker thought he should stir it up, "What I tell ya; Bob, this one means business. We got us a new sheriff." I tried to laugh it off, but, before I could properly diffuse the situation, Bob shot back in a slow deep voice, "This sheriff can be killed just like the last sheriff." Great, I thought, here we go again—another whacked out criminal to deal with.

Meth-Heads

After the tiger nearly killed my friend the animal keeper, I started to take the drug talk more seriously. That was when I realized just how dangerous the San Francisco Zoo was. I thought back on the day they wheeled that beautiful woman out of the dilapidated building called the Lion House. I thought about the people she had put her trust in: me for one, her fellow keepers, and the management. The keeper staff did not care much for this badly behaved group of maintenance people entrusted to keep the animals behind their bars and moats. And it was quite clear why. I don't know how it escaped me for so many months. Maybe they stayed away from drugs when I first started; that would have been a good idea with a new boss, but I just don't know for sure. Maybe I was too busy. Maybe I expected more out of the workers. But it was clear now that this whole group was really fucked up every day. I did not want to believe someone would come to a job like this high; it was so dangerous anyway. You would have to be an idiot, I thought, to risk your life and the lives of other people counting on you. I thought back to when Willy Ramirez relieved me of my work to clear the USDA violations on the tiger grotto walls, the way I pleaded with Willy not to take me off this important job, warning him and the director that the big cat could escape. I thought back on the workers left in the tiger's grotto as Tatiana the tiger violently ripped the flesh from this young mother's arms, just a 1/4" away, separated by a shift door maintained by these same drug using workers. I pleaded with the zoo management to do something about these workers: I wrote and recommended suspensions for these very dangerous workers but still, all they could say was, "Look at Mo. We need to discipline Mo."

Mo was the African American on the crew and the only one on the crew whom I felt was doing his job. I never suspected him of being on any drugs. I told the management that I would not be a part of any illegal preferential treatment or singling out of anyone on the basis of color. I thought back to my work with the City and County of San Francisco, and how this type of thing was so common in a supposedly progressive and diverse city. Every department I had worked in practiced institutionalized racism. Racism was so widespread and accepted that the practice of denying some people's basic employment rights was not even questioned: it was just the way it was. The same with the corruption: no one batted an eye at the stealing, the padding of timecards, the unchecked overtime, supervisors ignoring test results and manipulating the system to the point that you could finish number one on a city test and never get the job.

A few days after the terrible attack on the keeper, Willy Ramirez invited me to a managers' meeting at the old director's house at the San Francisco Zoo. This old 1920's building held a great deal of emotion for me. When I was a small kid my brother and I would sneak behind the gates and look at this house with awe and envy. The director of the zoo was given this small residence by the City and County to live in while he worked at the zoo. This particular director had children, and their bicycles and toys were strewn about the spacious lawn. How lucky these kids were to live at the zoo. I often wished I was them.

Now, years later, invited and part of the team, I entered this old house and I looked around. What a mess, I thought: the roof was falling apart and the spacious lawn was covered with tools and broken car parts. The gardeners had moved in. The little palace gem was worn, unkempt and filthy. One of the kid's bedrooms was turned into a locker room for the city workers. An old guy dressed in a zoo uniform flicked the hot ash from his smelly cigar on the antique hardwood floor as I walked by. I joined the other managers at the long, vintage dining room table. I looked down at the chairs; they were new, and had rollers that had notched the fragile floor. Willy Ramirez, the thirty-year old wonder boy, sat at the head of the table. I sat to his right. Across from me were the I.T. people: Ken and Mona. Next to them was Jen Long, an unpleasant woman who had developed a strong dislike for me, mainly because I accused the people she hired of using drugs. Jen was exceptionally angry at this meeting. Jen Long was the safety officer at the zoo, and she was responsible for emergency drilling and preparation. In the eight months I was at the zoo, we never had an emergency drill, and boy, did it show when Lea was mauled. Next to Jen Long sat Chaz Lonnet, a shining example of a San Francisco City and County worker.

Chaz had no supervisor at the zoo. Officially, Chaz was a gardener foreman—an area supervisor they call it. Chaz was left over from when the city ran the zoo. Chaz Lonnet did exactly what he wanted, which was absolutely nothing. Well, almost nothing: Chaz Lonnet was in charge of the gardeners and tree trimmers. There are a lot of trees at the zoo, and they fall all the time. If you didn't ask just the right way, a fallen tree would stay in your work area for years. Chaz Lonnet was a bastard, and everyone at the zoo disliked him immensely. But if you did not kiss his ass, you could be put in grave danger. Chaz wielded his power like a polished suppressor: the staff and the public were held hostage by this arrogant, angry, small man. Next to Chaz sat Paddy, the catering manager. He was a nice enough fellow, but prone to angry outbursts. And, of course, my baby talking boss, Candy Shultz, sat directly across from me, gazing over at me throughout the entire meeting, smiling and batting her eyelashes.

The tiger mauled the keeper on December 22, 2006. This meeting was about three days later. First on the agenda was a direct order from Willy Ramirez, C.O.O., for all managers to try to come up with new ideas for revenue generation. I thought this strange, but we all went through the motions, just like we did when we wanted a tree removed from the walkways or work areas. Next on the agenda was the tiger attack. First, Willy warned that the zoo was still trying to sort out the details, but he was interested in getting the managers' input. The group sat silent. Not a word as our leader scanned the pale and frozen faces. Willy got to me, and I cleared my throat. Jen Long's stare stung like sunburn on my face. The chef and caterer looked down in boredom.

I stated that I was on the other side of the zoo and I called the ambulance, but why had no one called 911 at or near the scene of the accident? "The workers you removed from my supervision were left in the grottos as the attack occurred, and afterwards I did not get them out until Lea was removed from the zoo. And by the way, what were you doing during the rescue? I did not hear you on the radio at all, Willy." "What I was doing or where I was at is none of your business," Willy spoke loudly. "Now wait just a minute, Lloyd," Jen Long screamed. "We saved her life: my people know what they're doing." I said, "Your people? We nearly lost this worker—the whole thing was a fiasco," I exclaimed. "At 5:00 p.m. the day the keeper was nearly killed, I went to the hospital to see if Lea was all right. Willy Ramirez called me after 5:00 p.m. and simply said: 'Where are you?' I told him I was at the hospital checking on Lea. Willy did not ask how she was; all he said was, 'Who else is there? Please remove your zoo jacket and make sure no one talks to the press.' I said okay and hung up. As far as the maintenance crew goes, three of them went directly to the scene, which was counter to the procedure. I was told the other worker made sure he could not be found."

When everyone calmed down at the meeting, I said, "We have an opportunity to examine this situation and learn from our mistakes." This set off another tirade from both Jen Long and Willy Ramirez. Just as I was sure the two of them were going to throw me out of the meeting, Ken, the ex-cop, spoke up: "What Lloyd was saying is true; we should look at this horrible experience and use this to better our response and fine tune our procedures." This pretty much ended the conversation, but not the hatred Willy Ramirez and Jen Long held for me. The meeting was called to an end rather quickly, and Jen Long stopped speaking to me. Willy Ramirez did not stop speaking to me; a few days later we had a cold spell at the zoo, and our gas heaters were all shut off. The animals were freezing and no one knew what to do. Willy Ramirez came to me and asked if I could figure this problem out. I said okay and negotiated a pressure increase from PG&E. This took several days. We then had to reset all the heaters and monitor the regulators for failure when the pressure was increased. I worked twenty-three days in a row to rectify the heating problem.

Since Lea had been injured, I found it hard to sleep. I was coming to the end of an extended shift when I started to notice the maintenance crew acting strangely. I turned my attention to them. My best worker was flying so high on speed he could hardly speak. I made contact with whichever two or three workers came to work on any given day. This day, there was only one. It was late January 2007. After seeing his condition, I quickly asked the individual if there was any reason he was not fit for duty that day or if he was sick. He assured me he was not sick as he rearranged his tools over and over again, moving his jaw back and forth rapidly, all the time sweating profusely and talking to himself. I asked this worker to please stay in the shop and not use any tools. I then went directly to the human resources director to get some guidance on the official policy for this type of situation.

The human resources director, Randy Moore, was not available. His assistant asked if she could be of some help. I wasn't sure if I should discuss this with anyone but Randy, so I declined to share and went back down to the dilapidated barn, which was also used as the storeroom for the steam train, where this worker welded. By this time he looked worse: chain smoking, dropping parts, and muttering to himself. We were scheduled to work on the 6,000-pound rhinos' safety doors today, then the tiger cages, and this worker was rearing to go. "Are we go,go,gog,gog,gog going to fix those safety doors, boss?" the whacked-out worker stuttered. I felt this couldn't wait; I told the welder to stay put and don't do anything, and went back to the director's office.

"Still not available," I was told by the human resources generalist, Bertha Dunne. I told her I had an emergency and it could not wait. The human resources director was another example of what you don't want in an employee, much less a senior manager. This director regularly boasted about the women he had fucked, although he was married and brought his family to the zoo often. He did not seem to mind bragging about his many conquests. In one out-of-the-blue lunchtime rant, he suddenly exclaimed, "I fucked all my students." I could not quite believe this admission, so I asked him to repeat this boast to the C.O.O., Willy Ramirez, which he did. This piece of non-fiction was meant to defuse the situation with my supervisor Candy, who now was mounting a full campaign to discredit me and turn what managers she could against me.

Around this time, the chief operations officer, Willy Ramirez, started his campaign to deflect my allegations of sexual harassment against Candy Shultz. The San Francisco Zoo and Candy Shultz were found to have discriminated against a worker who had some disabilities. The E.E.O.C. required the zoo to pay Peter the pothead some money. The thing that really pissed the management off was the mandatory training the zoo had to supply to all supervisors. I was included in one of the sessions.

After a brief and bizarre opening monologue by Randy Moore about how winning is everything with human resources work, we all sat silent for Olivia the lawyer. Olivia spoke for several hours regarding reasonable accommodation, and what was, and was not, reasonable. Having some experience with this complicated law, during question and answer time I raised my hand. Our featured speaker did not seem to understand my question and I was told to see her after the talk.

This I did, waiting in line with several other supervisors who also had questions. I felt someone close to me and turned to see Willy Ramirez, the second in command at the zoo, smiling slyly. As I moved closer to the young woman, Willy began to speak. "Her ass, her ass. What about her tits?" I couldn't quite believe our operations officer had said this. We were a couple of people away from the lawyer. I shot him a nervous look and whispered, "What?" Another question was answered by our smartly dressed guest and the line moved forward. I was about three feet from this young lady when our thirty-year old wonder boy exclaimed again, "Her ass, her ass. What about her tits?" Having heard this, the attorney turned red. As my turn came next, I asked some question regarding the Americans with Disabilities Act and then I left as quickly as possible. The only way I could figure this out was Willy and Randy were working very hard to trivialize my situation with the winking Candy.

Finally, I could wait no longer. It was nearly 11:00 a.m. and the twitchy worker was getting jumpy. This particular worker had been disciplined previously for an angry outburst. Another time when I directed this worker and others to return to their work areas, he became upset, removed his gloves, and asked me to step outside, raising his voice at me. I then asked Bertha when Randy would be available, reiterating that this was an emergency. "Please, Lloyd, let me help you. What seems to be the problem?" I told her I had an employee who was extremely high and I needed some guidance on the zoo's procedure. "Oh! Well, let's see Lloyd, we will look in the zoo employee's manual." We did this together and could not find anything, other than employees are not allowed to come to work under the influence of drugs or alcohol. The funny thing was there was no language on what to do when an employee was under the influence. The manual does state that a worker can drink alcohol at work if they have permission from their supervisor. "Sorry I couldn't help you, Lloyd. I will tell Randy you are looking for him," Bertha said casually. Crazy place, I thought.

I returned to the broken-down barn were the worker was nervously rearranging the tools and muttering. I asked him to come outside. It was nearly noon now. I wanted to get in plain view, just in case this whacked out cretin took a swing at me. At least there might be someone around to call an ambulance. I wasn't too optimistic after the fiasco with the tiger keeper. I told my best worker that I believed he was on drugs and he was to punch out before he hurt himself or someone else, and not to come back to work until he was straight and sober. The worker apologized and admitted he had used drugs and quietly left the grounds. I was relieved, and disappointed in our human resources director, but not surprised.

A couple of days later the worker had not returned, but his wife had. She was fucked up. The talkative maintenance worker was higher than a kite as well, and both shot me a hateful look. I asked the smallish fellow to stay put and please not to perform any work. I then asked the young woman to accompany me around the zoo for my inspections. She was silent but followed me.

My charge really looked bad. Large open sores covered her face, her eyes were bloodshot and running, her nose was a bright red, with liquid running down to her mouth. She wiped the liquid with her dirty and ripped sleeve. Her clothes were unwashed and torn. I asked her if there was any reason she could not work today. She was mumbling and fidgeting, then suddenly, she broke down in tears. This worker started to yell, then to cry. She got mad, walked away, then came back and screamed, "Why!" I asked her if she was on drugs, and she exclaimed, "I do not know why you are picking on us; we have been your best workers, the others do way more drugs than me and Jimmy." I asked, who does what drugs? The very high maintenance worker stated, "Peter and Mo do way more drugs than we do, usually meth and weed." I told this worker I would check it out and I told her to leave the zoo grounds and to stay off the grounds until she could come to work sober.

I stopped by the shop area on my way back to the damp, moldy office trailers. Peter the weed smoker and resident troublemaker stared at me and smiled a very stoned smile. I asked Peter if was he high on anything? Peter smiled again and said, of course not. I wasn't sure. He must have gotten some Visine, because he did not look as bad as before, and I was exhausted.

Now, it had been two days and I still had not heard from our fornicating human resources director. I assumed I was on my own with this problem. I had written a report after the first incident. I had called and left a message with the director. I had even told his assistant that I was very upset and I was considering an incident report complaining about the H.R. guys' failure to participate. I went back to the zoo office and the worker I had just told to leave the grounds was in my office. I asked her what she was doing there and she said she had been to the human resources director's office, and was told she did not have to leave the grounds, and she was going to work. She shot me a sly, over the shoulder smile, and walked slowly out of my office. I was surprised—and it was hard to surprise me. The extremely dangerous work these employees performed, the danger the public is put in, the danger the animals are in—I could hardly breathe.

A few days later when my office phone rang, I answered and a familiar voice spoke, "Lloyd, this is Bertha. Could you please come to my office?" Sure, I said, and made my way over to the leaking, mold filled trailers the zoo had purchased some years ago for the administration staff. I had tried to fix the problems and even rid one trailer of all its problems, but when I reached $15,000 dollars I was told by Willy Ramirez to stop the work. The San Francisco Zoo director asked for a report on the remaining ten trailers; I told him they were filled with mold and they posed a danger to the workers and the public. The Director of the Zoo stated, "If the workers don't like it, they can work somewhere else." I walked into Bertha's office. She asked me to shut the door, which I did. The smell of mold was mixed with the stale aroma of cheap perfume.

"I need you to leave Renee and Jimmy alone; we need these two to testify against this other worker we fired." I was flabbergasted. I knew the administration was mostly incompetent boobs, but this, this was too much. I calmly said, "Look Bertha, this I can not do. These people could kill someone or harm themselves." I told Bertha that one of them was working on the black rhino enclosure and the other on the great ape enclosure. We had a grave situation and Randy needed to get involved. Bertha stated, "This comes from the top—leave these workers alone." I told Bertha I wasn't going to do that, and I left her office. I drove out to Lake Merced, right across the street from the San Francisco Zoo, and stared blankly at the water I so loved, drifting into memories of the past.

Chapter Sixteen

Tatiana

I was making my rounds in early February of 2007 when I came by Tatiana the tiger's grotto. It was early in the morning. I don't know if the keepers were there yet. The big cat stared at me from across the moat. She paced and kept her eyes on me as I slowly walked by, pacing and measuring me as I moved. A wave of panic shot through my body as she crouched and readied her powerful legs. I looked around the rotten enclosure: broken concrete was exposing the reinforcing steel bars. The cracks in the walls ran with water and moss and grass grew out from the short walls.

I thought back on the morning I met with the San Francisco Zoo director Carlos Casseris and Willy Ramirez, the operations officer. "We need more time and money for these grottos," I said. "What do you mean Lloyd; you have already spent more than you were authorized to on the first one," Willy said with a smirk. Carlos stared at the crumbling walls. "How much more money you need, Lloyd?" Carlos asked. Willy quickly went to note taking mode. I told the two that we needed to get the U.S.D.A. out there to inspect what we had done already and see just how far they would like us to go in order to satisfy their citation. Willy Ramirez looked up from his notepad; Carlos sent him a troubled look. We all stood silent for a few seconds, until Carlos finally said, "Under no circumstances are you to call the U.S.D.A. or invite them here for any reason. Is that clear, Lloyd?" Carlos put his head down and started to walk away. Willy was close behind, jotting things in his notebook as they walked away. I walked quickly to catch up. I stopped in front of the two and made eye contact with both. "This tiger can get out of here," I said, pointing at Tatiana's enclosure. "Hell, I could get out of here," I continued. "You see those exposed bars? It's like a ladder. You see those cracks and grass growing out of the moat wall? Most animals stay in their enclosures because they want to," I said.

Ask any zoo professional: many in our captive animal population could walk, jump, or fly right out of their pens. They just don't want to; the outside world scares them. They are institutionalized; they are afraid of the outside. All they have known is captivity. Tatiana was different though. She was born in captivity, but she had just enjoyed some freedom a few months ago. Not real freedom, but freedom of spirit. She bit the hand that fed her, these weak, two legged, hairless creatures that kept her captive. One had gotten too close and she took full advantage, ripping the flesh from her jailer.

Willy came to my office a few hours after our meeting in front of Tatiana's grotto. "I am taking you off the grotto work, Lloyd," Willy Ramirez exclaimed. "Oh, no, why?" I asked. "I don't have to give you a reason, Lloyd," Willy shot back, like a five year old. "But I will tell you this, Lloyd—Carlos did not appreciate your wanting to call the U.S.D.A. We have got rid of a lot of people here for not being team players. Carlos and I have plans for you, big plans, if you could be more of a team player."

I tried to concentrate on the terrible mistake they were making by taking me off the cat and bear grottos. I had spent months getting bids, interviewing concrete contractors, and geo-technical firms. It took a great deal of effort to coordinate the work in these grottos. There was only a ¼" steel door separating the workers from the tiger, lions, and bears. These doors were maintained by the absolute worst trades-people I had ever seen—and I had worked around trades-people all my life. I had gotten entire measurements of all the grotto's wall, heights included, and handed them over to senior management. "I want you to tell Candy this is her job now." "You want me to tell her," I asked. "Yeah, you tell her," Willy Ramirez, our thirty year old superstar, said in a deeper than usual whine.

I had not slept a full night since Lea was mauled. Worries about the drug abuse, the investigations of me, and human resources ignoring the grave concerns I had with the animal enclosures kept me from relaxing. I wrote and wrote discipline requests. The workers, I thought, were the biggest threat to safety, and every time my requests were ignored. These workers posed a threat to the public, themselves and the animals that was hard to ignore. "If you knew that the worker who kept the lions from killing you was so high he couldn't hold a tool, how would you feel about the zoo?" I asked Willy Ramirez. I got a blank stare from the chief operations officer at the San Francisco Zoo. A blank fucking stare!

The big cat grottos and the bear grottoes were falling apart. The black rhino could walk right out of his enclosure any time he so chose. And, to top it off, the people the public counted on to keep the animals in their enclosures were so high they could hardly speak. Open drug dealing was done on zoo grounds; this was a mad house, a real zoo. Willy Ramirez spoke, "I need you to pay the worker you sent home for being high." I asked Willy if he would push for a tighter drug policy. He did not answer me, but the next day I was given notice we were to have a meeting on the new drug policy. This new drug policy was extremely unpopular, as you would guess. Drug users hate drug policies. And the drug users hated me, my crew, and the crew I depended on in very dangerous situations.

I knew about drug policies: Muni had a drug policy, a tough one. I thought back on my time at the cable car barn. Now the drug policy at the cable car barn looked tough, and officially it was. If you got in an accident or anyone was hurt on your cable car you were taken immediately to the drug-testing center. This policy was followed for the most part. This was followed so well because most of the operators were black. But there was another prong as well; all of the maintenance personnel had to be tested randomly. And random it was not. Certain well-

connected people were never tested. I was there for nearly five years and many people were never tested. Others
were tested and tested. The only people who were termi-
nated for drug or alcohol use were either black or female.
My boss shot heroin and snorted coke: he was promoted
but never tested. Another mechanic smoked weed all day:
never tested. The Municipal Railway or Muni was, and
is, a twisted place.

My zoo cell phone interrupted my walk down memory
lane. It was Jen Long, the operations manager. An enemy
of mine now, she was extremely upset with me for complaining about the safety response.

Exposure: that is what terrifies a city worker. With
the botched response to Lea's injury, the workers she had
hired and coddled now had a drug policy to adhere to.
The operations manager was being exposed for what she
really was: an inept supervisor, a bad judge of character, and an uncommitted worker only concerned with her
own paycheck. "Lloyd, what are you doing," Jen asked
in a panicky voice. "Jen, I am in a meeting now," I said.
"Click." Jen was gone.

We did not speak until the day I left. The new policy
was not as tough as I would like. If a worker was thought
to be on drugs or alcohol they were to be sent to the
human resources office. Human resources would decide if
they were to be tested. From the surface this looked fine,
but we had already gone through that. I was told not to
report certain workers because they were needed to testify against other workers. I felt this place falling apart.
The San Francisco Zoo was too dangerous of a place to

have people high and working, for any reason. I felt I was next to get hurt here and started planning to leave. I did not want to. I love the San Francisco Zoo and I dearly wanted to help right the sinking ship.

I composed an improvement plan outlining what had to be done to straighten out this madhouse and sent it to the director. Apparently, my direct supervisors got hold of it, because the next day I was summoned to a meeting with the C.O.O. Ramirez. After my complaint back in October 2006 regarding my supervisor requiring me to spend my lunch times with her and walk around with her, the zoo had started to investigate me as well.

It was more irritating than threatening. This fifty-year-old woman was constantly inviting me to her office to eat lunch, offering me her lunch, and relating gossip on the sexual activities of our coworkers. Candy really wanted to go off campus, she would say, and have a "real lunch." She would then ask about the nearby drinking establishments and had I ever been to any of them. This woman seemed lonely, above all else, and I sort of felt sorry for her. I had to ask the French fellow who had had my job previously to please stay out of Candy's office, as he would spend hours in there with the door closed. I was extremely short handed. I said I needed him on his task and not in our supervisor's office. I spoke to Candy as well: she agreed he had no business up in her office, and coyly agreed to decline his visits. When I approached Jacques on the matter of his long visits to Candy's office, he stood straight and in a French accent he warned me to, "Stay out of his and Candy's relationship. It is personal, and if you know what's good for you, you will butt out." I told this surly Frenchman that I was not concerned with his personal relationships but during work hours he was to be at his assigned post. The worker laughed and walked away. My supervisor's constant advances were making it hard for me to get my work done. I told her I would not be joining her for lunch, but I would be happy to meet with her anytime during the regular workday. This did not sit well with my amorous boss. When my probation was up and I was to receive my evaluation, which I hoped would spell the beginning of my pay increase, I was told that if I did not consent to these dates I would be denied my raise and would not pass my probation. I had had just about enough of this nonsense, and I told her so. I told the facilities manager at the San Francisco Zoo that this type of behavior is sexual harassment and she should know that. We agreed to meet again and she repeated her requirement and marked me down for not having lunch with her. I was about at the end of my rope at the zoo. I brought this requirement to the attention of the human resources director Moore, who promptly told me to get a lawyer. I did not, but I wrote a rebuttal and took the issue to Willy Ramirez. This angered our little Caesar and he promptly doubled my duties and put me under his charge.

Even though the zoo came out on my side on the sexual harassment, they must have thought they needed some leverage on me. So they interviewed the workers I had accused of drug use, and they let the other two workers know I was recommending discipline proceedings for them. As you can imagine they had nothing nice to say and I was disciplined for using bad language and harassing these employees. I objected to this retaliation and Randy Moore told me if I did not sign this discipline, "It would go far worse for me." I thought back over the times I had had with the City and County.

"Well, are you going to sign this?" Moore demanded. "Willy, I fear if he doesn't sign this discipline, things will get worse for Lloyd." Willy Ramirez was thinking hard. Willy knew I was his bread and butter. A tremendous amount of work was completed in my short tenure at the zoo. Willy liked the fact I had changed out the contractors who were charging the zoo three and four times construction industry standards. I had the sewer department back online with the zoo after several years of neglect. Candy couldn't help insulting the city workers and they hated her for these slights. As it turned out, the boss of the sewer department was an old friend of mine and the crews would come out and clear our lines at a moment's notice. I had the City Plumber producing and the City's Recreation and Park department helping out as well. This took a great deal of ass kissing on my part. Every time the sewer department would help us out I would make sure they got all they could eat at the zoo restaurant and I made sure they did not have to pay. I also was able to award these folks with free passes to the zoo for their friends and families. But mostly, I think they liked all the women that were at the zoo, so they were happy to come out. And, as it turned out, with all my years and troubles with the City and County of San Francisco, I had become sort of a legend, you might say.

The stories were tall about me, and I did nothing to dissuade the attention and adulation I received from the new generation of city workers. We fixed water lines that had been broken for as long as some workers could remember; we worked on the new exhibits and fixed their long standing problems. I was able to involve the animal staff in the decisions on what to fix and what could wait. My predecessor wielded her power much like any city boss; if you did not show the proper respect or if you did not ask nicely, you and your zoo work were forgotten about, for years sometimes.

The city plumbers and I fixed a water leak that had been leaking for twenty years. It had leaked so long a wetland was created that held a great deal of wildlife. The story I got was the female keeper refused the advances from the maintenance boss at the time and the leak was never fixed, so this worker had to perform her dangerous work with a wetlands in the middle of her area. The keepers were happy with the changes I was making and Willy knew this. He might have been young, but he was not stupid. I worked every day and I was on call 24/7. If he got rid of me he would upset people. And that would mean more work for Willy. He did not like work, at least not zoo work.

Willy Ramirez spent most his time working his other job. Willy had a consulting firm that was based in Mexico. Willy would spend hours and hours on the phone to his partners trying to garner amusement park deals all over the world. Willy had also let me in on many of his and the zoo's secrets. I often wondered why, when I would get a radio call for maintenance or repair from the workers at the Lion House, Willy would either call me on the zoo radio or have me meet him at his office, come to my office, or call me on my zoo cell phone, checking to see what the cat keepers wanted. Willy then would tell me that, "We have many more pressing needs, and the Lion House is not one of our priorities." Finally, after one of his many uncomfortable interrogations on the needs of the big cat animal keepers, I asked little Caesar, "Why I am not to fix the problems at the Lion House?" I was surprised again at Willy Ramirez's explanation.

I was told by the chief operations officer at the San Francisco Zoo that, "The Director of the Zoo and the Zoological Society Board of Directors need the Lion House to continue to deteriorate to the point that another tax bond can be voted in." I did not know what to say. Another crazy idea, I thought. Do these people have any idea what they are doing? Then I said, "Willy, you can't be serious." Willy grew angry, like he usually did when his orders were questioned. "Look Lloyd, Carlos is the only one that's keeping that Lion House open; most people want it closed or tore down." I kept quiet this time and left this pompous criminal's office.

The Zoo Director was happy with my work. Carlos gave me a large bonus right around the time I had complained about my supervisor Candy Shultz wanting me to go out with her. I thought that strange, and Carlos wrote glowing email reviews about my work and my talent for "getting things done."

My thoughts returned to the present as Willy Ramirez answered the pushy human resources director. "Let's see Randy; let Lloyd look this over and we will talk again tomorrow." I thought back on my interviews for this job at the zoo. Candy Shultz, Willy Ramirez and Randy Moore interviewed me. All three thought it best that I work to fire most of the maintenance crew. At the very least, the black guy, who was the lowest paid, and the Chinese plumber. As the months passed I found these were my best workers. Having seen the inaccurate account on these workers I asked my new boss, why should I want to fire these better than average workers? Candy said, "I feel it is more of a cultural thing, Lloyd." I know what that means.

The only worker off limits was the former supervisor, who by the way was the worse employee I had ever encountered in forty years of working. This worker claimed to be French. Although I didn't really care, I thought this not to be true. During my first month on the job I was invited to a discipline hearing involving some illegal pay Candy Shultz had awarded this dangerous and ill-qualified worker. I do not know why I was asked to attend, as both Jacques and Candy resented me for witnessing their admonishment. As it was explained in the hearing, Candy Shultz, the former maintenance supervisor, had requested a large raise for Jacques. This was turned down by the human resources department due to union rules. Candy gave the worker the money anyway and now the zoo was demanding the worker or Candy pay back the overage. This worker presented the zoo with many challenges.

First and foremost, this worker had a strong disdain for the zoo, and worked very hard to sabotage any effort to better the enclosures and make the zoo safe for the public and workers. I wrote this worker up and recommended swift action to avert some tragedy, but from the time I arrived to the day I left, I was not allowed to discipline this extremely disruptive worker. Candy pleaded with me to ease up on this man, and stated more than once that she had a "great deal of affection for him." The French, accident-prone worker echoed this sentiment many times. I told Candy and the rest of the senior staff what a danger this worker was to himself and others. Because I could not discipline this worker, I tried to give him work that would not pose a danger. But Jacques would find some way to make it a danger.

I was at the end of my rope: I was not allowed to discipline the drug users; I was not allowed to discipline the incompetent workers who posed a threat to the public and the animal collection; and I was being disciplined for doing what I was supposed to do. And, I was turning fifty years old in a few days, working seventy-five hours a week for $65,000.00 a year. I was fearful we would have another terrible accident like Lea's. How could we not have another accident with this group of incompetent, stoned workers, coupled with a detached management interested only in revenue generation and their own careers? I would probably be the one who would be killed.

I went to Willy Ramirez; I told him my concerns. I told Willy the frustration I had. I told him the hours were too long and I had much more work than time. Willy stated I could not discipline the workers I had recommended but I could work to fire Mo the black man. Willy offered me a $20,000.00 a year raise and a promotion. I asked if I could take some time off to think about it.

I went to my best thinking place, the Duke of Wellington Pub on Portobello Road in London, England. I thought long and hard. I went to the Eiffel Tower. My wife and I discussed our options while sipping French champagne. I returned to the zoo in two weeks and on February 19, 2007 I resigned my position. I was sad to leave my zoo. I thought I could help and I did for a short time. I changed a few things, but the zoo would have killed me before I could fix it. I couldn't forget the zoo though, and I grew bitter as the sleepless nights multiplied.

I got another job but I couldn't concentrate. How had these horrible people dared run me off from the job I had dreamed about my whole life? I was worried about the people there: the animal keepers and the visitors, even the ones who drove me from my job. I did not want them hurt. I wanted them to get help; they were only the product of this corrupt and badly run institution. I felt guilty for leaving them. I thought about the tiger grotto and the bear grotto crumbling around these dangerous animals. I thought about the beautiful black rhino fruitlessly trying to protect his mate by charging the endless cement trucks coming and going. I thought about the construction across from the lions and tigers, the fear these animals had of the loud, smoky machines invading their small spaces. I thought about Candy withholding the repairs on these enclosures to punish the workers who stood by me. I thought of my daughter: a zookeeper. I began to panic.

In April of 2007 I called the E.E.O.C. and lodged a complaint against the zoo. I told them of the impending escape of the big cats and bears. They referred me to Cal OSHA. In July of 2007 I called Cal OSHA and told them of the many violations at the San Francisco Zoo. I spoke with the district manager and the inspector who found the zoo at fault for the keeper's mauling. They admitted they were fearful of animal escapes. "But we really do not know much about zoos," the busy manager admitted. "We leave these issues to the zoo." I warned them of the tiger escape and they apologized for their lack of knowledge and bid me goodbye. In September of 2007 I emailed the San Francisco Board of Supervisors. I told my district supervisor I needed to talk to him immediately, that I was the former maintenance supervisor at the San Francisco Zoo, and I felt the public and the animals were in grave danger.

In November of 2007 my lawyer and I had a meeting with the Zoological Society's lawyers and my old friend Randy Moore. I told this room full of lawyers that the zoo was the most dangerous place I had ever worked. I told them the tiger would escape and the bears too. I told them the rhino pen was rotten and he was bound for a short stint at freedom. My lawyer repeated this to them and said, "And when it happens, he would make sure the press knew of this meeting." The lawyers for the zoo looked bored. "We are not afraid of adverse publicity," the lawyer in charge stated and promised another meeting.

We never had one.

On Christmas Day, when I heard of the young man's death, I was not surprised. Terribly sad and disappointed, but not surprised. Most workers at the zoo were not surprised either. Tatiana had measured her pen, just as I did. Tatiana the tiger left her prison because she could. And for a brief time she was free—free to do what she so enjoyed—ripping the flesh from the hairless beings she so hated, once again. And the same zoo manager who had screamed at and berated me in front of the managers for questioning the safety procedures locked the other two defenseless and bleeding men from safety. The zoo presented her with a commendation for bravery. These same brave people had mounted an attack on my character as I labored day and night to keep the animals from freezing, doing what no one else could or would do.

The zoo began a campaign to discredit the young men. The zoo hired an ex City Attorney and a well-known spinmaster to pollute the eventual jury pool, saying they were high or drunk. They were not as high or drunk as the people charged with keeping that animal in its grotto. The zoo said the young men had done terrible things. The zoo and this despicable team of high priced spin doctors said they brought this attack on themselves. The zoo kept a nine-foot animal behind twelve-foot walls. They ran machinery practically next door to this animal for over a year, day in and day out, huge earth moving equipment, cement trucks belching smoke rambling loudly by these shy carnivores. Everyday scores of loud and untrained construction workers were taunting these animals. For

Tatiana there was nowhere to go. The Lion House, her home, was filled with more of these creatures, looking for a good show at feeding time. What a living hell these creatures have. How could you be surprised this beautiful animal left her enclosure? Any fate would have been welcome other than the dismal reality of her pitiful existence.

Tatiana escaped her prison and died in a hale of gunfire. She made one last charge at the uniformed men with guns. Tatiana knew about uniformed men with guns. Doctor Death wore a uniform and used a tranquilizer gun. All the big cats were paralyzed with fear of the man in the uniform and the dart gun. But this time it was different for the big female tiger. Tatiana had a choice. Instead of leaving her victims and running back to her cell of horrors in fear, she crunched the bones of these defenseless men. The men lay bleeding in front of a locked café, left to die by the fleeing workers, locked safely in their warm stores.

Tatiana faced the blue men who meant to kill her and in one last blast at freedom she left her bloody conquests and charged her killers. Tatiana was shot point blank in the head as she leapt into the only freedom she had ever known—death. A beautiful cat born into captivity, fed at the pleasure of her jailers, her rations cut so she could put on a better show for the people who claimed to love her. This cat knew what we all know. It is better to die on your feet than live on your knees.

Tatiana was a victim; victims victimize. There was no good reason for this tiger to kill Carlos, other than the fact that she could. Humans are weaker than tigers, so tigers kill and eat humans. That's it, nothing more— it's that simple. I've come across people who take advantage of other people for no other reason than they can. I've met people who are unfair to people of color. They are not racist, they just take advantage of people they can. Blade Manish broke my back. He is not necessarily the animal he appears to be. The Blade took advantage of me because he could—it's human nature. Big Daddy stole the city blind because he could. We allowed him to, just like we allow the zoo to operate in the nonsensical way it does. The animals have not finished escaping. The chimps will grow tired of the torment they endure each day. The giant flightless birds will get a hold of a keeper or a child soon enough, again. The bears will find their way out of the dilapidated grottos some time soon, and for the big cats behind the rotted wire mesh, it is just a matter of time.

About the Author

Lloyd Kraal is a licensed General Building Contractor with over twenty-five years of experience, specializing in construction management. He is currently a small business owner under contract with several local government agencies. He has estimated or managed 100 million dollars in construction work and evaluated over 1,000 employees and subcontractors. He teaches classes on construction estimation and acts as a small business consultant. He has been married for twenty-seven years and has three grown daughters. Along with his wife he has owned and operated a restaurant and a catering company. In his free time he enjoys oil painting, travel, and being outdoors.